Fate and Faith after Heidegger's Contributions to Philosophy

FATE AND FAITH AFTER HEIDEGGER'S CONTRIBUTIONS TO PHILOSOPHY

PETER S. DILLARD

PICKWICK *Publications* · Eugene, Oregon

FATE AND FAITH AFTER HEIDEGGER'S CONTRIBUTIONS TO
PHILOSOPHY

Pickwick Publications
An Imprint of Wipf and Stock Publishers
199 W. 8th Ave., Suite 3
Eugene, OR 97401

www.wipfandstock.com

PAPERBACK ISBN: 978-1-5326-6233-1
HARDCOVER ISBN: 978-1-5326-6234-8
EBOOK ISBN: 978-1-5326-6235-5

Cataloguing-in-Publication data:

Names: Dillard, Peter S., author.

Title: Fate and faith after Heidegger's contributions to philosophy. / Peter S. Dillard.

Description: Eugene, OR : Pickwick Publications, 2020. | Includes bibliographical references and index.

Identifiers: ISBN 978-1-5326-6233-1 (paperback) | ISBN 978-1-5326-6234-8 (hardcover) | ISBN 978-1-5326-6235-5 (ebook)

Subjects: LCSH: Heidegger Martin—1889–1976. | Theology.

Classification: B3279.H49 D55 2020 (paperback) | B3279.H49 D55 (ebook)

Manufactured in the U.S.A.   03/11/20

In memory of my mother, Mary Alice Dillard

"Don't play what's there; play what's not there."

MILES DAVIS

Contents

Introduction

In Search of a Theology of *Streit*

DISPATCHES FROM HIGHER GROUND

IN THE SUMMER OF 1927, shortly before the publication of *Sein und Zeit*, Heidegger wrote to his friend and colleague Karl Jaspers:

> I'm off to the cabin—and am looking forward to a lot of strong mountain air—this soft light stuff down here ruins one in the long run. Eight days lumbering—then again writing. . . . It's late night already—the storm is sweeping over the hill, the beams are creaking in the cabin, life lies pure, simple and great before the soul. . . . Sometimes I no longer understand that down there one can play such strange roles.[1]

Throughout Heidegger's career, the famous cabin or *Hütte* at Todtnauberg served as a kind of intellectual fastness from which the philosopher pursued his own original thinking with Zarathustrian detachment. Yet if Heidegger thought that the people at the lower elevations were behaving strangely, then with equal justification they could have said that he was certainly jotting down some very odd things up there in his refuge at the edge of the dark forest.

For example, in his *Beiträge zur Philosophy (Vom Ereignis)*, a philosophical *Denkbuch* of private entries he kept between 1936 and 1938, Heidegger writes:

---

1. Heidegger, *Briefwechsel*, 53, quoted in Sharr, *Heidegger's Hut*, 63.

1

> The last god *essentially occurs* in the intimation, in the intrusion and remaining absent of the advent as well as the absconding of the gods that essentially occur as having been [*gewesend*] and of their concealed transformation. The last god is not the event itself and is yet in need of the event as that to which the one who grounds the "there" belongs.[2]

Here, Heidegger sketches part of the basic narrative presented in the *Beiträge*. In "the first beginning" of Western philosophy, the early Greek thinkers—including Anaximander, Heraclitus, and Parmenides—experienced being non-metaphysically as an upsurge (φύσις, *physis*) of beings emerging and tarrying for a while before passing away. Originating in the philosophy of Plato and Aristotle, continuing through the philosophies of Descartes, Leibniz, Kant, and Hegel, and culminating in the perfectionistic voluntarism of Nietzsche, being becomes metaphysically misunderstood as the maximally general characteristic common to all and only beings. The "event" (*Ereignis*) or "the other beginning" (*der andere Anfang*) is a possible future transformation of Western thinking, whereupon being will no longer be conceptualized but instead will be understood in a radically non-metaphysical manner that is preserved in appropriate language, artworks, and deeds. Only then might the advent of "the last god" occur, whereby the holy or divinity manifests itself through a decision reached by human participants who ground the non-metaphysical event of being in the "there" of their own temporal-spatiality.

Heidegger's enticing talk of the last god prompts the question of what, if any, relation the discourse of divinity in the *Beiträge* and subsequent works bears to theology. A particular proto-theological picture begins to take shape based on the *Beiträge* narrative itself. The divinity that might be revealed post-metaphysically in the last god is not the same as any specific being, non-being, or the non-metaphysical event of being (what Heidegger calls "beyng"): "The god is neither a 'being' nor a 'nonbeing' and also is not to be identified with *beyng*."[3] Heidegger claims that the last god "needs" the non-metaphysical event of being: "Beyng attains its greatness only if it is recognized as that which the god of the gods and all divinization *need*."[4] But he also implies that there is a correlative sense in which the non-metaphysical event of being "needs" the last god in order to become divinized, since

---

2. Heidegger, *Contributions to Philosophy*, 324.

3. Heidegger, *Contributions to Philosophy*, 207.

4. Heidegger, *Contributions to Philosophy*, 192.

it is the god "who *pervades* beyng *with divinity* always only in work and sacrifice, deed and thought."[5] Non-metaphysical being's need to become pervaded with divinity sheds some light on why Heidegger denies that the last god is a non-being like Santa Claus or the Easter Bunny, since the latter are mere fictions incapable of bestowing divinity or anything else upon the non-metaphysical event of being. Nevertheless, the emerging proto-theological picture remains unsatisfyingly vague, since so far it lacks any connection to concrete human experience.

In order to fill this lacuna, it is instructive to reflect upon two different kinds of phenomenological description found in Heidegger's later philosophy—including, but not restricted to, the *Beiträge*. Especially in his writings from the 1930s, Heidegger foregrounds what he calls the struggle (*Streit*) between world and earth: the striving on the part of human beings engaged in the various activities that make up their existence to wrest unconcealment, clarity, and disclosure from concealment, hiddenness, and obscurity.[6] Heidegger's writings from the 1940s until the end of his career shift away from the earlier emphasis upon struggle towards a serene "letting-be" (*Gelassenheit*): a tranquil yet energized dwelling that encompasses and preserves the "fourfold" of earth, sky, divinities, and mortals.[7] Depending on how these different phenomenological descriptions are assigned to the relevant parts of Heidegger's *Beiträge* narrative, two theological options become apparent as ways of fleshing out the proto-theological picture. If we experience *Ereignis* as an intense struggle to wrest non-metaphysical clarity from metaphysical obscurity, whereas we encounter divinity as an energized tranquility, then a theology of *Gelassenheit* becomes possible. Conversely, if we experience our liberation from metaphysical confusion as a peaceful state of energized tranquility, while we encounter divinity as something hidden, enigmatic, or even paradoxical with which we must

---

5. Heidegger, *Contributions to Philosophy*, 206.

6. "Only if self-concealing reigns throughout all the realms of production, creation, action, and sacrifice by weaving them together in an essential occurrence, and if self-concealing determines the clearing and thus at the same time essentially occurs by encountering what secludes itself within the clearing, only then does *world* arise, and at the same time (out of the 'simultaneity' of beyng and beings) the *earth* springs up" (Heidegger, *Contributions to Philosophy*, 276).

7. "In saving the earth, in receiving the sky, in awaiting the divinities, in initiating mortals, dwelling occurs in the fourfold preservation of the fourfold. To spare and preserve means: to take under our care, to look after the fourfold in its presencing" (Heidegger, "Building Dwelling Thinking," 151).

struggle in order to attain some measure of illumination, then one might choose to pursue a theology of *Streit*.

In a recent study, the rudiments of a non-metaphysical *Gelassenheit* theology rooted in the Christian faith tradition have been developed.[8] Human beings experience the non-metaphysical event of being as a piecemeal and incremental struggle to gain a foothold of thoughtful openness by unraveling metaphysical and other kinds of philosophical misconceptions that distort our understanding of divinity. The stage is then set for the human encounter with the holy as something purportedly "out there" and real that is neither any specific being nor the non-metaphysical event of being but rather a pervasive energized tranquility. The interplay between the contrasting elements of energy as unsettled agitation and tranquility as satisfied yearning within the overall phenomenon of divine *Gelassenheit* can then guide us to accept, reject, or ignore actual or possible changes of which we have become aware in the situation of thoughtful openness.[9] The aforementioned study also explores ways in which our encounter with the holy as *Gelassenheit* can be integrated with Christian commitments to the Incarnation, the Atonement, the Indwelling of the Holy Spirit, and the Trinity construed in a decidedly non-metaphysical light.[10]

But what of the other theological option described above? What reasons might be given for developing a theology of *Streit*? Within the broad framework of Heideggerian non-metaphysical theology, theological alternatives are crucial not only as a means of promoting fruitful dialogue but also in order to demarcate sharply between faith and theology. If there is only *Gelassenheit* theology, then faith as it is conceived in the Heideggerian framework threatens to collapse into *Gelassenheit* theology itself. It would then follow that no one can be a sincere person of faith unless she is a *Gelassenheit* theologian. Any such conclusion is thoroughly unacceptable. Simply having faith in the way that a child has it does not require one to embrace any particular theology, even if in some contexts the theology in question might contribute to a better understanding of what one faithfully believes. On the other hand, if the same faith can also be articulated in terms of *Gelassenheit* theology, *Streit* theology, and possibly others as well, then faith itself stands out as the common denominator of all these theologies, and thus as something autonomous that is not reducible to any one of

8. See Dillard, *Non-Metaphysical Theology after Heidegger*.

9. See Dillard, *Non-Metaphysical Theology after Heidegger*, 113–30.

10. See especially Dillard, *Non-Metaphysical Theology after Heidegger*, 131–66.

them.[11] The situation is then analogous to the plurality of more traditional theologies such as Thomism, Scotism, Calvinism, and process thought, whose contemporary adherents should also be encouraged to interact critically with the emerging Heideggerian theological framework.

However, there is an even deeper reason for pursuing *Streit* theology in a non-metaphysical Heideggerian setting. Most conspicuously in its phenomenological account of how the holy is capable of guiding human decision-making, *Gelassenheit* theology assumes that human beings can gain immediate experiential access to the holy presence in a situation of thoughtful openness. Only then may the interplay between the elements of energy and tranquility within the experience of *Gelassenheit* reveal whether an actual or possible change of which one has become aware should be embraced, rejected, or ignored. How does the holy become experientially available to us in the first place though? A casual reader might get the impression that according to *Gelassenheit* theology, we gain phenomenological access to the holy merely through succeeding in our piecemeal struggle to overcome various conceptual confusions that cloud our thinking about divinity. Once these blinders are removed, we then immediately encounter the holy. Yet rigorous analysis aimed at deconstructing metaphysical and other philosophical misconceptions is a purely intellectual activity. At least as Christianity and the other monotheistic faiths conceive the fullness of divinity, we do not simply think our way to God.

Theologians like Martin Luther would put the point even more bluntly. Original sin is a pervasive and corrupting influence that blinds our thinking, experiencing, and other natural capacities to the presence of divinity. Thus we find ourselves not in a situation of thoughtful openness to God but instead in the predicament of being radically alienated from Him. The idea that we, in our fallen state, can somehow make decisions guided by our experience of the holy is naïve intellectualism at best, dangerous heresy at worst. If there is some other path around the deleterious consequences of original sin into an intimate dwelling with the divine, the *Gelassenheit* theologian does not say what it is.

Interestingly, from the perspective of Heidegger's *Beiträge* narrative concerning the non-metaphysical event of being and a possible epiphany of the last god, *Gelassenheit* theology gets things exactly backwards. Heidegger writes:

11. This point is made in Dillard, *Non-Metaphysical Theology after Heidegger*, 72.

> But beyng essentially occurs as event, the site of the moment of decision regarding the nearness and remoteness of the last god. This *transformation* [via the non-metaphysical event of being] creates the space of the other necessities for the decision regarding the nearness and remoteness of the gods.[12]

There is much in this passage that is obscure, but one point is crystal clear. If Heidegger is right that remote divinity in the form of "the last god" or "the gods" only draws near to us through some sort of decision we must make once we have undergone the transformation to a post-metaphysical situation, then obviously our decision here cannot be guided by our experience of immediately accessible divinity. For it is only through the decision itself that we might experience an epiphany of the holy, a theophany.

What has been said so far suggests that Heidegger's *Beiträge* might be a valuable resource for the project of developing a non-metaphysical *Streit* theology that (1) distinguishes divinity as such not only from any specific being but also from the non-metaphysical event of being and (2) identifies our fundamental encounter with divinity as a struggle to find clarity in the face of obscurity. Nevertheless, the task of mining the *Beiträge* for possible theological insights is a formidable one. As can be seen from the few passages that already been quoted, it is a daunting, perhaps even impregnable text. We need to find a path into the *Beiträge* that, although it does not presume to offer a comprehensive interpretation of Heidegger's difficult work, provides us with a definite orientation so that as theologians we can absorb its main ideas and effectively engage the relevant issues it raises. The somewhat circuitous route we shall take begins with an earlier text by Heidegger.

Walking a Tightrope between Philosophy and Theology

Shortly before his departure from Marburg University in 1927, Heidegger delivered a lecture eventually published as the essay "Phenomenology and Theology."[13] The topic of the lecture is the precise relationship between Christian theology and phenomenological philosophy as entirely different sciences, each with its own posit (*positum*) and distinctive methodology. Heidegger begins by distinguishing ontic sciences, which are concerned with specific beings, from ontological science, which is concerned with

---

12. Heidegger, *Contributions to Philosophy*, 181–82.
13. Heidegger, "Phenomenology and Theology," 39–62.

being per se.[14] The *positum* of theology is "Christianness," a historical mode of individual and communal human existence (*Dasein*) that its faith participants—including the theologian herself—believe to reveal a specific being: "For the 'Christian' faith, that being which is primarily revealed to faith, and only to it, and which, as revelation, first gives rise to faith, is Christ, the crucified God."[15] To the extent that theology deals with a specific being, then, it is an ontic science resembling chemistry, mathematics, and zoology, each of which deals with specific beings of various kinds.[16]

However, unlike these other ontic sciences, the goal of theology according to Heidegger is not to acquire a body of knowledge but rather to bring greater transparency to faith through a conceptual interpretation that neither justifies faith nor makes it any easier but actually make faith harder:

> The specific content of the object of theology demands that the
> appropriate theological knowledge never take the form of some
> free-floating knowledge of arbitrary states of affairs. Likewise, the
> theological transparency and conceptual interpretation of faith
> cannot found and secure faith in its legitimacy, nor can it make it
> any easier to accept faith and remain constant in faith. Theology
> can only render faith more difficult, that is, render it more certain
> that faithfulness cannot be gained through the science of theology,
> but solely through faith.[17]

Thus theology is the ontic science of conceptually self-interpretive faith in the crucified God that is made increasingly more difficult through this very activity of conceptual self-interpretation.

Phenomenological philosophy, by contrast, is regarded by Heidegger as the ontological science *par excellence*, since it is not limited to any specific being or range of beings but investigates the nature of being as such.[18] Heidegger proceeds to delineate the interrelations among faith, the ontic science of theology, and the ontological science of philosophy in terms of a set of dependencies and independencies. Unless it seeks to become self-reflective, faith does not needs the conceptual interpretation of it provided

14. See Heidegger, "Phenomenology and Theology," 41.

15. Heidegger, "Phenomenology and Theology," 44. For Heidegger's introduction of the term "Christianness," see 43.

16. See Heidegger, "Phenomenology and Theology," 41, 48.

17. Heidegger, "Phenomenology and Theology," 46.

18. See Heidegger, "Phenomenology and Theology," 41, where Heidegger speaks explicitly of "*the* science of being, the ontological science, philosophy."

by theology.[19] Furthermore, faith does not need philosophy; indeed, Heidegger goes so far as to claim that "*faith*, as a specific possibility of existence, is in its innermost core the mortal enemy of *the form of existence* that is an essential part of *philosophy* and that is factically ever-changing."[20] The alleged conflict between faith and philosophy will be the topic of the next chapter. For its own part, philosophy needs neither faith nor theology, since the philosopher can conduct a phenomenological investigation of being per se without believing in the crucified God or engaging in conceptual reflection on this religious belief. Finally, as conceptually self-reflective faith, theology obviously needs faith. Theology also needs philosophy, since theological concepts take for granted at least some initial understanding of being per se, the *positum* of philosophy as ontological science. For example, Christian theology operates with the concept of *sinful existence*, which in turn includes the ontological notion of *existence* as one mode of being per se. Hence by providing what Heidegger calls friendly "co-direction," the phenomenological investigation of being may clarify or even correct the concept of existence presupposed in theology.[21]

The present study will develop a non-metaphysical Christian theology of *Streit* that takes the framework of "Phenomenology and Theology" as its point of departure and utilizes the *Beiträge* as its primary philosophical resource. We will see how there is a dialectical path leading from the initial receptivity to Christian theology in Heidegger's writings from the early to mid-1920s, through the increasing hostility to faith and theology in *Sein und Zeit* and other works by Heidegger in the early to mid-1930s, to the surprising resurgence of quasi-religious language and themes in the *Beiträge*. Immediately, the approach that has just been outlined faces three *prima facie* objections. The first concerns the latter work; the other two pertain to the earlier essay.

The first objection is that even though the *Beiträge* contains enigmatic references to the gods and the last god, Heidegger remains staunchly opposed to any Judeo-Christian understanding of divinity, insisting that the

---

19. At one point, Heidegger even floats the possibility of faith without theology: "If faith would totally oppose a conceptual interpretation, then theology would be a thoroughly *inappropriate* means of grasping its object, faith" (Heidegger, "Phenomenology and Theology," 45). This possibility will be further explored in chapter 2.

20. Heidegger, "Phenomenology and Theology," 53.

21. "The theological concept of sin as a concept of existence acquires that correction (i.e., co-direction) that is necessary for it insofar as the concept of existence has pre-Christian content" (Heidegger, "Phenomenology and Theology," 52).

last god is "the god wholly other than past ones and especially other than the Christian one."[22] Elsewhere in the same text Heidegger elaborates:

> This unfolding of the *first* end (in Platonic-Aristotelian philosophy) of the first beginning makes it possible that this Platonic-Aristotelian philosophy and, in *its* form, henceforth Greek philosophy in general could then provide the framework and foundation for Judeo-Christian (Philo-Augustine) faith and from this point of view could even be taken as a forerunner of Christianity, precisely as the "paganism" that has been overcome.[23]

For Heidegger, Judeo-Christian faith is rooted in a philosophy that sometimes is more Platonic (e.g., with Philo of Alexandria or Saint Augustine), at other times is more Aristotelian (e.g., with Saint Thomas Aquinas), but is always thoroughly metaphysical. Thus with the radical overcoming of all metaphysics envisioned in the *Beiträge*, Judeo-Christian faith must also fall by the wayside. Perhaps in a radically post-metaphysical world there will be some kind of theophany, but whatever god or gods are revealed there will have nothing whatsoever to do with the personal God of the Jewish and Christian faiths.[24]

This objection has a short answer and a longer one. The short answer is that we should not automatically assume with Heidegger that all Christianity is essentially a creature of metaphysics. The earliest Christians were largely, if not entirely, innocent of any Platonic, Aristotelian, or other kind of overt metaphysical speculation. The idea that they were nonetheless tacitly entangled in the "metaphysics of presence" that Heidegger believes has dominated Western philosophy from Plato until today needs to be justified rather than merely presupposed. The longer answer will have to wait until chapter 8, where decidedly Christian resonances in Heidegger's engagement with the poetry of Georg Trakl will become evident. To be sure, Heidegger strenuously disavows the presence of any "Christianity" either in Trakl's poems or in his own commentary on them. It will be argued that, despite Heidegger's protestations to the contrary, considerations intrinsic to the non-metaphysical outlook of the *Beiträge* motivate a decidedly Christological interpretation of the last god and its possible epiphany.

---

22. Heidegger, *Contributions to Philosophy*, 319.

23. Heidegger, *Contributions to Philosophy*, 165.

24. Vallega-Neu clearly formulates this objection in her *Heidegger's "Contributions to Philosophy*," 102.

The second objection returns to an aspect of the position set forth in "Phenomenology and Theology." Recall that Heidegger identifies the cruci- fied God as the particular being that is the *positum* of theology as an ontic science. Any such identification conflicts with a central contention of the proto-theology that emerges from the *Beiträge* narrative and serves as the common ground between the theologies of *Streit* and *Gelassenheit*: namely, the divinity manifested in the last god is not any specific being. Since the framework of "Phenomenology and Theology" *does* take divinity to be a specific being, it cannot serve as a suitable basis for developing a *Streit* theology that draws upon the philosophy of the *Beiträge*. A cogent reply must work out a plausible account of how the crucified God as something transcendent escapes total identification with any specific being, yet as something intimate enjoys a special intimacy with a specific human being. This work will be the focus of chapters 3 and 8.

The third objection to our envisioned development of a *Streit* theol- ogy zeros in on another claim Heidegger advances in "Phenomenology and Theology," according to which faith and philosophy are fundamentally incompatible. If theology is nothing other than self-reflective faith seek- ing greater transparency through a conceptual interpretation, then it fol- lows that philosophy is also incompatible with theology. But then, contra Heidegger in 1927, philosophy cannot offer theology any "co-direction" by clarifying ontological concepts presupposed by theology, since philoso- phizing requires entirely abandoning the faith commitment that is essential to theology. The same is true where the philosophy is that of *Sein und Zeit*, *Einführung in die Metaphysik*, or *Beiträge zur Philosophie*. Formulating the most serious version of this objection in the next chapter will set us on the previously mentioned dialectical path through the possibility of theology without philosophy, the possibility of philosophy without theology, and the possibility of a *Streit* theology co-directed by and completing the philoso- phy of the *Beiträge*.

The Plan of the Present Study

Chapter 1 scrutinizes the objection that philosophy is fundamentally in- compatible with theology. Upon closer inspection, we will see that there are less and more serious versions of the incompatibility objection. The most serious version is that the incompatibility stems not from an opposition of basic attitudes or from a divergence in methodology but rather from a genuine ontological conflict between Heidegger's existential phenomenology in *Sein und Zeit*, which takes the experience of *Angst* to reveal human being-in-the-world as an essentially finite mortality terminating in death, and the Christian theological view of human existence as continuing beyond death either in intimacy with God or in alienation from Him. Once this ontological conflict has been brought into proper focus, it then becomes possible to examine and evaluate different responses to the incompatibility between philosophy in the form of Heideggerian existential phenomenology and theology grounded in the Christian faith.

Chapter 2 considers one extreme response to the incompatibility: namely, the theologian might try to bring greater transparency to her increasingly difficult faith through a conceptual interpretation that makes little or even no use of philosophy. By returning to Heidegger's own engagement in the early to mid-1920s with the thought of St. Paul and Martin Luther, we can begin to see how someone might begin to develop this kind of response. Its chief drawback is that the paucity of philosophical resources available to Heidegger during this phase of his career prevents him from resolving serious theological conundrums both with Paul's eschatology and Luther's view that human nature has been totally corrupted by original sin. Thus it is not surprising that Heidegger moves away from theology toward the richer phenomenological and philosophical perspective culminating in *Sein und Zeit*. A last-ditch, Luther-inspired proposal to make theological paradox or even theological contradiction criterial for divinity is also weighed and found to be unsatisfactory. For the foregoing reasons, the possibility of a non-metaphysical *Streit* theology without any philosophy whatsoever is set aside. The question then arises of which philosophical resources are best suited for the successful execution of our project. We will return to this issue in chapters 4 and 5.

Heidegger's increasingly anti-religious turn, beginning with the officially agnostic approach of *Sein und Zeit* and culminating in the avowedly atheistic stance of *Einführung in die Metaphysik*, points toward another extreme response to the incompatibility objection: specifically, Christian theology informed by faith might be repudiated in favor of pure Heideggerian existential phenomenology. Chapter 3 challenges the presumed religious neutrality of Heidegger's philosophical perspective. Some recent efforts aimed at uncovering religious presuppositions of Heideggerian phenomenology are first reviewed and judged to be unsuccessful, though suggestive. A new, internal critique centered on the methodologically key experience of *Angst* is then presented with an eye to revealing the tacit theological content of Heidegger's phenomenology in the late 1920s, the early 1930s, and even beyond. Briefly, the noetic stability of anxiety across ontologically distinct noematic contexts (*Angst* in the face of uncanny human being-in-the-world, an uncanny particular non-human being, the uncanny totality of beings, the uncanny non-metaphysical event of being, and uncanny absolute nothingness) reveals the purported intentional correlate of anxiety as something distinct from all of these phenomena. This distinct something is the holy, "the last god," or simply God. Yet exactly why our encounter with various uncanny non-divine phenomena is also an experience of anxiety before divinity remains unclear.

Its avowedly post-metaphysical stance, together with its willingness to broach quasi-theological themes such as the status of the prophetic "future ones" and "the absconding or passing by of the last god," makes the *Beiträge* a possible philosophical resource for developing a non-metaphysical theology of *Streit*. Chapter 4 serves as an entry point into Heidegger's challenging text by scrutinizing its attempt to think of being non-metaphysically as something other than the maximally general characteristic common to all beings. Clear instances of how interdependencies between new human identities and new kinds of non-human beings first emerge when a definite commitment is undertaken give us some grip on what Heidegger has in mind. Unfortunately, his vision of a single, monolithic "event" (*Ereignis*) in which beings come to "shelter" interdependent *Da-sein* and non-metaphysical being threatens to collapse into an empty tautology. It is then argued that Heidegger's notion of "time-space" restores definite content to the monolithic event, but only at the cost of reinstating metaphysics. The main conclusion of chapter 4 is that the specific commitment of having to decide about the absconding or the passing by of the last god within the event is indispensable to the *Beiträge*'s attempt to think being both non-tautologically and non-metaphysically.

Chapter 5 opens by explaining how some ideas found in the *Beiträge* can be fleshed out in order to resolve the Pauline and Lutheran conundrums mentioned earlier. For example, by pushing the *Beiträge* ideas of time and history in a more theological direction, the historical Jesus himself and the episodes of his life may be viewed as a special kind of sacred clock against which other historical happenings can be measured as early or late but whose own "strokes" or movements—including Christ's eventual return at the *parousia*—are neither early nor late but simply unfold. Additionally, the *Beiträge* idea of contemporary human being (*Dasein*) as enmeshed in a "plight," combined with the Kierkegaardean-inflected idea of a "leap" into genuine selfhood (*Da-sein*) that has yet to occur, gestures toward a conception of original sin not as the total corruption of human nature but as a ubiquitous and deleterious condition preventing human beings from making essential decisions that would allow them to become genuine selves. A recent discussion of irresolvable moral quandaries helps to elaborate the new conception. These preliminary results confirm the importance of the *Beiträge's* philosophical perspective for working out a theology of *Streit*. Chapter 6 concludes by showing how this same philosophical perspective nevertheless places us in the intolerable theological predicament of having to make a pivotal decision about the absconding or passing by of the last god that we have absolutely no clue how to make. The upshot is the deeply religious *Angst* described earlier, where the various non-divine phenomena phenomenologically available to us strike us as uncanny precisely because they still fall short of the unavailable God we are still somehow responsible for reaching.

Chapters 6, 7, and 8 then appraise three distinct theological proposals for overcoming this predicament. Each proposal builds upon philosophical concepts set forth in the *Beiträge* and related writings.

Chapter 6 picks up on Heidegger's concept of absence as a kind of presence. To overcome the theological predicament, it might be proposed that our religious anxiety of having to make a decision about the last god we have no idea how to make is assuaged by the realization that the last god's remoteness or concealment from us is, paradoxically, precisely the way in which the last god draws near to us into disclosure. The nearness-in-remoteness theological proposal has affinities with Nicholas of Cusa's vision of God as a coincidence of opposites, Luther's conviction that God's wisdom and power are revealed as hidden under their opposite forms of folly and weakness, and, more generally, the tradition of apophatic theology. The proposal's main weakness is that the notion of divine nearness-in-remoteness is too vague to distinguish the revelatory situation in which the last god really passes us by in a genuine theophany from the non-revelatory situations in which although we wait for its arrival the last god absconds by remaining absent, or even from the apathetic situation in which no longer wait for the last god but simply forget all about it. Because it renders the phenomenon of the holy completely empty, the nearness-in-remoteness proposal is unsatisfactory.

Chapter 7 takes its departure from Heidegger's provocative remarks about the phenomenon of nothingness. Heidegger describes how nothingness can play a creative role, as when the inner recess or void of a jug allows its walls to come together to form the vessel. Nothingness can also play a delineative role, as when the interior of an ancient Greek temple *in situ* brings the surrounding landscape into sharper focus, or a captivating role, as when we are drawn into a gathering in the open space of a forest glade. Sometimes nothingness plays all three roles simultaneously, as when the vault of the temple allows its walls and roof to come together, sharpens our awareness of the surrounding landscape, and draws worshippers inside to participate in a sacred rite. Theologically, the union of creative, delineative, and captivating dimensions in a single threefold nothingness that serves as an integral counterpart to particular non-human beings, *Da-sein*, the totality of beings, and the non-metaphysical event of being has obvious Trinitarian overtones. Since our experience of nothingness is not fraught with anxiety but instead charged with purpose and fulfillment, identifying triple nothingness with the holy seems to escape the predicament of not knowing how to make a decision we nonetheless must make. Even so, the relation of modality to divine nothingness remains troublingly ambiguous in the *Beiträge*. Heidegger wavers between (1) inconsistently elevating possibility and necessity to foundational metaphysical principles governing relation between the non-metaphysical event of being and nothingness, and (2) insisting that all modality is grounded non-metaphysically within the event while never explaining how. This unresolved ambiguity makes the divine nothingness proposal unacceptable.

Using some of Heidegger's reflections on thinking and the poetry of Georg Trakl as a springboard, chapter 8 crafts a Christological proposal for overcoming the theological predicament of experiencing *Angst* over having to decide about the last god without knowing how to decide. The proposal unfolds in a series of stages. First, "the splendor of the simple" is interpreted as an initially enigmatic placeholder for the divine as a holy superabundance that is intimately unified with *Da-sein*, any particular non-human being, the totality of beings, the event of being, and nothingness. Anxiety then gives way to what Heidegger calls "trembling," the exciting realization that in encountering any of the aforementioned non-divine ontological conditions we are already encountering God as the splendor of the simple. Immediately the question arises of why divinity does not coalesce with the various non-divine ontological conditions with which it is intimately united, resulting in a monism totally at odds with the Christian commitment to divine independence. In order to preserve the real distinctness of the holy superabundance, Heidegger's notion of "pain as the converse" inspired by the poetry of Georg Trakl is invoked in connection with the phenomenological dynamics of the Crucifixion: in His superabundance, God fully pervades while also standing over against and beyond each of the ontological conditions described by Heidegger. The impossibility of making a decision about divinity is replaced with the intensifying trembling of the faithful, each of whom attains genuine human selfhood by perpetually hunting down God abiding in, in converse opposition to, and conversely beyond her thrown human existence. The chapter also considers how the Christological proposal understands the relation between divinity and modality, including the possibility of our liberation from original as well as all other forms of sin.

The purpose of chapter 9 is to counteract a pair of obstructive tendencies that threaten to undermine the emergent Christological theology of *Streit*. One such tendency is the apparent incompatibility between the core conceptions of *Streit* theology and the laws of nature uncovered by natural science. The role Heidegger assigns to strangeness and uniqueness enables us to resist the slide from science into scientism by distinguishing the replicable initial conditions upon which any scientific law or principle is based from a non-replicable, strange, and unique situation in which the last god emerges. A second possible obstacle is Heidegger's favoring of German over other languages as "the house of being" inhabited by Hölderlin, Heidegger himself, and "the future ones of the last god." This linguistic chauvinism tends toward a form of linguistic predestination that reinstates crippling anxiety before an inscrutable deity, since we can never be entirely sure whether we are speaking the right language in the right way required for the "inceptive thinking" practiced by the elect. Through a careful analysis of Heidegger's stress on the interdependency between inceptive language and *Da-sein*, the problematic metaphysical conception of language latent within this elitist tendency is deconstructed.

The concluding chapter revisits the contrast between the theology of *Streit* and the theology of *Gelassenheit*, arguing that several potential disadvantages with *Streit* theology that have been previously noted are avoided by the Christological version of that theological option developed in this book. Some possible lines of future inquiry are also identified.

Before proceeding with the various tasks outlined above, a word about the spirit in which the present work is written is in order. Ignored by much of contemporary philosophy and suffering from an intense identity crisis, Christian theology today stands at a critical juncture. Either it can retreat into strident, bunker-style apologetics that preaches to the choir while otherwise falling on deaf ears, or it can become increasingly self-involved and esoteric to the point of withering away into total irrelevance for most people of faith, or it can co-facilitate its own extinction as an autonomous discipline by allowing itself to be appropriated by secular and partisan political agendas on either the Right or the Left. Fortunately, there is a fourth possibility: in trenchant dialogue with Heidegger's challenging perspective in the *Beiträge zur Philosophie*, Christian theology might illuminate both promising as well as problematic aspects of this philosophy while developing its own fresh and distinctive voice suitable to an era marked by bewilderment in the face of information overload, cultural malaise, and cancerous apathy. Somewhat poetically expressed, the theology developed here seeks to be a spring wind of insight blowing through gray trees that seem dead yet perhaps are only sleeping, and so might one day reawaken.

Chapter 1

The Seeds of a Conflict

Faith is so absolutely the mortal enemy that philosophy does not even begin to want in any way to do battle with it. This *existentiell* opposition between faithfulness and the free appropriation of one's whole Dasein is not first brought about by the sciences of theology and philosophy but is *prior* to them. Accordingly, there is no such thing as a Christian philosophy; that is an absolute "square circle."[1]

A PICTURE AND A PUZZLE

WE BEGIN BY RECALLING the basic picture of the relationship between theology[2] and philosophy that Heidegger presents in his 1927 Marburg lecture "Phenomenology and Theology." Theology is an ontic science that takes a specific being—Christ, the crucified God, who is revealed through faith—as its topic. The methodology of theology is to bring greater transparency to faith in the crucified God through a conceptual interpretation that renders faith more rather than less difficult. Philosophy, on the other hand, is the ontological science that investigates the nature of being per se. The kind of philosophy Heidegger has in primarily mind is phenomenology, the methodology of which is the careful and accurate description of the manifold phenomena we experience with an eye to elucidating the fundamental

1. Heidegger, "Phenomenology and Theology," 53.

2. Unless otherwise indicated, "theology" henceforth designates Christian theology. The intent is not in any way to disparage non-Christian theologies but merely to streamline the text.

phenomenon of being itself. Despite their thematic and methodological differences, and despite the fact that philosophy does not require any assistance from faith, Heidegger urges that philosophy can assist theology by clarifying ontological concepts the latter discipline takes for granted.

Immediately, Heidegger's insistence in the same lecture that faith is the mortal enemy of philosophy seems to call the foregoing picture into question. If faith is incompatible with philosophy, and if theology is nothing other than self-reflective faith seeking greater and more challenging transparency, then it appears to follow that theology is also incompatible with philosophy. But then *prima facie* it is puzzling how philosophy could contribute anything to theology rather than undermine it, since to philosophize is presumably to abandon the faith that is essential to theology yet irreconcilable with philosophy.

The force of the puzzle turns on the answers to the following questions. Is there really a conflict between phenomenological philosophy and faith in the crucified God? If so, then what sort of conflict is it? Does the conflict in question constitute a genuine incompatibility that precludes theology informed by faith from consistently accepting any phenomenological clarification of ontological concepts presupposed in theology? As will become evident below, one sort of conflict between faith and philosophy does not prevent philosophy from contributing to theology. Moreover, there is a way of construing phenomenology that leads to no conflict whatsoever between phenomenological philosophy and faith. Perhaps for these reasons, then, it is understandable how Heidegger in 1927 can speak favorably of "the *possibility of a community of the sciences* of theology and philosophy."[3] It is only when philosophy is identified with the distinctive existential phenomenology set forth in *Sein* und *Zeit* that an apparently insurmountable incompatibility arises between philosophy and faith that prevents any community or peaceful coexistence between philosophy and theology. We must pinpoint the source of this incompatibility in order to lay the groundwork for the analyses to be undertaken in subsequent chapters.

Clashing Attitudes and "Ontology"

One kind of conflict between philosophy and theology that is grounded in faith arises from the differing human attitudes towards life or, as Heidegger terms them, "forms of existence," associated with these respective

3. Heidegger, "Phenomenology and Theology," 53.

18

disciplines. A person who is committed to the philosophical form of existence exemplified by Socrates strives to live in such a way that he refuses to accept any belief unless it is either self-evident, logically deducible from self-evident beliefs, directly confirmed by experience, or perhaps part of a predictively successful scientific theory. A phenomenological philosopher may be particularly keen to base her results solely upon what is experientially available to us. On the other hand, a person who is committed to a faithful and, by extension, theological form of existence is willing to accept some beliefs as true based solely on the authority of scriptural revelation, perhaps mediated by sacred tradition.

The philosophical/phenomenological and faithful/theological attitudes toward life are certainly incompatible, since no one can adopt both of them simultaneously. Nevertheless, this clash of attitudes does not automatically preclude the philosopher from clarifying concepts employed by the theologian. To take a mundane example, the theologian who believes on faith that Jesus walked on water (Matt 14:22–33; Mark 6:45–51; John 6:16–21)[4] takes for granted the concept of linear motion, since for Jesus to walk from the shore to the disciples out in the boat requires him to be capable of moving in a line from one point to another. Without sharing the theologian's belief that Jesus walked on water, the philosopher could still provide "co-direction" by defending the possibility of linear motion against, say, Zeno's paradoxes. Or to take a more phenomenological example, the philosopher could carefully describe how different kinds of beings featured in this scriptural episode—things of nature like the wind and the waves, tools like boat with its sails and oars, and human beings—are given to us in experience without professing any belief in the miracle of Jesus's walking on water.

Another kind of conflict that might arise between philosophy and theology is not just a difference in attitude toward life but a substantive ontological disagreement either about beings or about the nature of being itself. Allowing philosophy to "co-direct" theology in ontological matters without also allowing theology to scrutinize philosophy's own ontological assumptions then comes across as objectionably lopsided. S. J. McGrath, who crisply articulates this objection, goes so far as to say that the Heidegger of "Phenomenology and Theology" is not "a facilitator of authentic theology, but rather something of a theological terrorist."[5] McGrath explains:

4. All biblical references are from the New American Bible.

5. McGrath, *Early Heidegger and Medieval Philosophy*, 177–78.

> Because a pre-Christian content inevitably enters into theology, philosophy's prerogative extends into theological terrain. Where philosophy retains the right to correct the ontological concepts presumed by theology, theology has no place critiquing the vision of human existence coming forth in philosophy.[6]

McGrath's point is that Heidegger loads the dice against theology in favor of philosophy. For although philosophy is free to correct or even to deconstruct the ontological presuppositions imported into Christian theology from pre-Christian sources (e.g., the ancient Greek concepts of substance, accident, and essence deployed in Scholastic theology), theology is not permitted to challenge any tendentious ontological claims set forth in philosophy. Theology must simply sit there and take it, so to speak.

To evaluate McGrath's criticism, it will help to clarify the term "ontology." W. V. Quine distinguishes between *ontology* as the particular entities to which a theory is committed and *ideology* as the stock of simple terms and predicates the theory contains.[7] Adapting Quine's distinction to our current purpose, we may say that two types of what can be broadly designated as an ontological dispute between the respective sciences of theology and philosophy as described by Heidegger in "Phenomenology and Theology" are possible. The first type of ontological dispute occurs when one of these sciences posits the existence of an entity *e* whose existence is denied outright by the other science. Here the theologian and the philosophy disagree about what there is. In the second type of ontological dispute, both sciences agree that *e* exists. Yet one science predicates something to be true of it ("*e* is P") that the other theory denies to be true of it ("*e* is not P"). Here the theologian and the philosopher have a dispute about what is true of something that they both take to exist.

With these considerations in mind, let us return to the relation between theology and phenomenological philosophy. Certainly theology as self-reflective Christian faith sets forth a definite vision of human existence that includes specific ontological claims, such as that God exists; that God became human in Jesus Christ; that Jesus suffered, died, and rose from the dead in order to offer redemption to humankind; that each human is created by God, eventually dies, and rises again, and then exists eternally

6. McGrath, *Early Heidegger and Medieval Philosophy*, 182.

7. See Quine, "Ontology and Ideology." In a later essay, Quine extends ideology to include perceptual capacities that are reliable indicators of various conditions (cats, sunsets, rain, etc.) even if subjects who possess these capacities lack any expressions for the indicated conditions. See Quine, "Ontology and Ideology Revisited."

either in intimacy with God or in estrangement from Him. Suppose that phenomenological philosophy sets forth conflicting ontological claims, either by denying the existence of some entity posited by theology, or else by denying some predicate to be true of an entity that theology affirms to be true of the same entity. Then undoubtedly the Heidegger of "Phenomenology and Theology" is biased in favor of philosophy against theology by allowing philosophy to criticize theology's ontological claims without giving theology the right of rebuttal.

The trouble is that it is hardly obvious how *phenomenological* philosophy makes any contentious ontological claims whatsoever; rather, it is only committed to describing as accurately as possible the phenomena of human experience. In his summary of the operational ground rules guiding the basic phenomenological orientation common to Husserl and Heidegger, Don Idhe observes:

> Thus, if phenomenology is not to founder at the very first step, it is essential that ordinary belief and taken-for-granted theory be suspended as far as to allow glimpses of what will be later seen more fully. Phenomenology calls on us to pretend that what we have as primary, as first given, are these immediate experiences, and to look carefully at them, perhaps more carefully than ever before. The first operational rule, then, is to attend to the phenomena of experience as they appear. A parallel rule, which makes attention more rigorous, may be stated in Wittgensteinian form: *Describe, don't explain.*[8]

By suspending ordinary belief, taken-for-granted theory, and all other attempts at explanation, phenomenology in at least the basic sense of the term refrains from making any controversial ontological claims about what does or does not exist beyond the phenomena that are given to us in experience. Phenomenology also declines to affirm what is true or not true of what exists, settling instead for ontologically more cautious observations concerning what *appears* to be true or not true of the phenomena we encounter. Consequently, depriving theology the right to criticize "the vision of human existence coming forth" in phenomenological philosophy doesn't really deprive theology of anything, since so far phenomenology as the ontologically neutral description of experience contains no definite

8. Idhe, *Experimental Phenomenology*, 18.

vision of human existence to criticize. Perhaps some more robust version of phenomenology does, but that remains to be seen.[9]

Might a conflict between phenomenology and theology arise not over what is or what is true of what is but over the nature of being itself? According to Heidegger's 1927 blueprint, the *positum* of theology is God, the divine being. In the *Beiträge*, Heidegger associates the divine being with a particular metaphysical conception of being endorsed by Judeo-Christian thought: "Even if a crude interpretation of the idea of creation is foregone, the fact that beings are caused remains essential. The cause-effect connection comes to dominate everything (God as *causa sui*)."[10] To be is to be caused. Non-divine beings are caused to exist by God, whereas God causes His own existence in the sense that the latter is a self-explanatory necessity, as for example St. Anselm argues. It might be thought that this theological conception of being stands at least potentially in conflict with whatever account of being per se is uncovered through phenomenological investigation.

However, Heidegger says something else in the *Beiträge* that blunts the edge of this potential conflict: "The god is neither a 'being' nor a 'nonbeing' and it is also not to be identified with *beyng* [the non-metaphysical event of appropriation]."[11] Here Heidegger is thinking of a post-metaphysical situation in which "the last god" who may either abscond or pass us by is not any specific being. In the previous chapter, we noted that this proto-theological picture is common to two possible non-metaphysical theologies: a theology of *Streit* and a theology of *Gelassenheit*. If the last god is not a being, then it is not a cause either of beings or of being itself. As avowedly non-metaphysical, neither *Streit* theology nor *Gelassenheit* theology endorses any metaphysical conception of being, including one according to which to be is to be caused, that potentially conflicts with the phenomenological investigation of being. While rejecting the idea of God as a specific being, both of these non-metaphysical theologies might still agree with Heidegger in

---

9. McGrath does claim that Heidegger's own existential phenomenology is not ontologically neutral: "Yet in the analysis of being-unto-death, the neural terrain of average everydayness is left behind, and one extreme ontic possibility of being-in-the-world is consulted for a clue as to how ontology can 'grasp' *Da-sein* 'as a whole'" (McGrath, *Early Heidegger and Medieval Philosophy*, 176). The next section will elucidate the precise character of Heidegger's non-neutral ontic analysis of being-unto-death. Chapter 3 will return to the question of how the theologian might effectively challenge it.

10. Heidegger, *Contributions to Philosophy*, 100.

11. Heidegger, *Contributions to Philosophy*, 207.

"Phenomenology and Theology" that their proper topic is divinity. Hence if there really is a substantive conflict between theology and Heidegger's understanding of phenomenological philosophy that makes them mutually incompatible, then to find it we must look elsewhere.

Essential Finitude

The vision of human experience that emerges from the existential version of phenomenology presented in *Sein und Zeit* most certainly *does* conflict with the vision of human existence lying at the heart of theology as self-reflective faith. According to Heidegger in his most influential work, human-being-in-the-world or "*Da-sein*" is ordinarily immersed in a variety of everyday projects. However, in rare yet deeply unsettling moments of anxiety (*Angst*), *Da-sein* comes face to face with its own existence as something uncanny (*unheimlich*).[12] What anxiety supposedly reveals to *Da-sein* is the essential finitude of its own existence, the fact that at its death it will cease to be entirely:

> In *Angst*, *Da-sein* finds itself *faced* with the nothingness of the possible impossibility of its existence. *Angst* is anxious *about* the potentiality-of-being of the being thus determined, and it discloses the most extreme possibility. Because the anticipation of *Da-sein* absolutely individualizes it and lets it, in this individualizing of itself, become certain of the wholeness of its potentiality of being, the fundamental attunement of *Angst* belongs to this self-understanding of *Da-sein* in terms of its ground. Being-toward-death is essentially *Angst*.[13]

Methodologically, the experience of *Angst* is integral to Heidegger's existential phenomenology in *Sein und Zeit*, since it is only through anxiety that the whole being of an individualized *Da-sein* in its entirety becomes revealed to itself as a theme for further phenomenological analysis.[14] *Da-*

12. For Heidegger's phenomenological description of the experience of anxiety see Heidegger, *Being and Time*, 170–79. It should be noted that although throughout the latter work Heidegger uses the term "*Da-sein*" to designate ordinary being-in-the-world that may either become authentic or remained inauthentic, the same term is used differently in *Contributions to Philosophy*. This difference in usage will be clarified in chapter 4. All occurrences of "*Da-sein*" have been italicized to mark that Heidegger is using it as a technical term.

13. Heidegger, *Being and Time*, 245.

14. For a clear exposition of this methodological point see Friedman, *Parting of the Ways*, 47–50.

sein may then choose either to exist authentically by embracing its own essential finitude in resoluteness (*Entschlossenheit*) or instead to lose itself in inauthenticity by joining the "they" (*das Man*) in covering up the radically individualizing character of death with empty generalities ("We all have to die some day") or metaphysical illusions ("Each person possesses an immortal soul").[15]

Both theology as the ontic discipline concerned with God in relation to human beings and phenomenology in *Sein und Zeit* as the ontological discipline seeking the meaning of being qua being through a proper analysis of *Da-sein* agree that human beings exist. However, theology predicates something to be true of each individual human being that *Sein und Zeit*'s existential phenomenology denies to be true of it: namely, theology asserts while phenomenology denies that each human individual exists beyond its own bodily death. Thus between these two disciplines there is clearly a substantive ontological dispute of the second type described in the last section. Theology's vision of human beings as created and then continuing after death to exist in relation to God is diametrically opposed to Heideggerian existential phenomenology's vision of human existence as essentially mortal and finite. Indeed, from the publication of *Sein und Zeit* in 1929 on into the 1930s Heidegger becomes increasingly aware of the fundamental opposition between theology and his own understanding of phenomenology.

Early on in *Sein und Zeit*, there is already a subtle shift away from the irenic perspective Heidegger had set forth in "Phenomenology and Theology":

> Theology is searching for a more original interpretation of human being's being toward God, prescribed by the meaning of faith itself and remaining within it. Theology is slowly beginning to understand again Luther's insight that its system of dogma rests on a "foundation" that does not stem from a questioning in which faith is primary and whose conceptual apparatus is not only insufficient for the range of problems in theology but rather covers them up and distorts them.[16]

Whereas previously it was suggested that philosophy can offer friendly "co-direction" by clarifying concepts presupposed in theology, now the implication is that theology's whole conceptual repertoire is woefully inadequate and obfuscating.

15. See especially Heidegger, *Being and Time*, 272–77.
16. Heidegger, *Being and Time*, 8.

In a similar vein, Heidegger complains:

> But what obstructs or misleads the basic question of the being of
> *Da-sein* is the orientation thoroughly colored by the anthropol-
> ogy of Christianity and the ancient world, whose inadequate on-
> tological foundations personalism and the philosophy of life also
> ignore.[17]

It is not so much that theology takes for granted ontological concepts that
need to be clarified but that theology is inextricably mired in ontological
confusions that must be extirpated if the proper phenomenological description of *Da-sein* is to proceed. Eventually, Heidegger explicitly draws
this very conclusion:

> The contention that there are "eternal truths," as well as the con-
> fusion of the phenomenally based "ideality" of *Da-sein* with the
> idealized absolute subject, belong to the remnants of Christian
> theology within the philosophical problematic that have not yet
> been radically eliminated.[18]

If there is some other, more transparent conceptual apparatus that is sufficient for the range of problems in theology, the Heidegger of *Sein und Zeit*
says nothing about it.

With regard to the specific issue of *Da-sein's* mortality, Heidegger's
official position is that the *Sein und Zeit* account of *Da-sein* as being-in-
the-world leaves open the question of whether there is life after death for
human beings:

> The ontological analysis of being-toward-the-end, on the other
> hand, does not anticipate any existentiell stance toward death. If
> death is defined as the "end" of *Da-sein*, that is, of being-in-the-
> world, no ontic decision has been made as to whether "after death"
> another being is still possible, either higher or lower, whether *Da-
> sein* "lives on" or even, "outliving itself," is "immortal." Nor is any-
> thing decided ontically about the "otherworldly" and its possibility
> any more than about the "this-worldly"; as if norms and rule for
> behavior toward death should be proposed for "edification." But
> our analysis of death remains "this-wordly" in that it interprets the

---

17. Heidegger, *Being and Time*, 45. Notice that here Heidegger no longer differenti-
ates between Christian theology and the Christian faith but lumps both together under
the term "Christianity."

18. Heidegger, *Being and Time*, 211.

phenomenon solely with respect to the question of how it *enters into* actual *Da-sein* as its possibility of being.[19]

Yet the supposed neutrality of Heidegger's phenomenological analysis does not square with its main methodological imperative. In order for the analysis to apply to *Da-sein* as a whole, the being of *Da-sein* must first be revealed in its entirety. As we have seen, *Da-sein's* experience of *Angst* in the face of its own death as the impossibility of its existence allegedly performs this disclosing function.[20] If there is something more to *Da-sein* beyond its own bodily death that is not revealed by *Angst*, then Heidegger's phenomenological investigation falls short of the total phenomenon of *Da-sein*. Thus in order to safeguard the comprehensiveness of his "analytic of *Da-sein*," Heidegger must insist upon *Da-sein's* essential finitude, and so he must repudiate the possibility of human existence after death. The ontological conflict between Heidegger's existential phenomenology and faith-grounded theology has become insurmountable.

By the time of his 1935 lecture series *Einführung in die Metaphysik*, Heidegger drops any pretense of phenomenology's compatibility with theology:

> Anyone for whom the Bible is divine revelation and truth has an answer to the question "Why are there essents rather than nothing?" even before it is asked: everything that is, except God himself, has been created by Him. God himself, the increate creator, "is." One who holds to such faith can in a way participate in the asking of our question, but he cannot really question without ceasing to be a believer and taking all the consequences of such a step.[21]

Heidegger denies that anyone can seriously engage in the kind of phenomenological investigation he is undertaking without abandoning faith in God and accepting the consequences of doing so—which includes giving up the Christian belief that each human being exists beyond her own bodily death in relation to God. Heidegger's existential phenomenology has moved from

---

19. Heidegger, *Being and Time*, 230.

20. "We conceived of death existentially as what we characterized as the possibility of the *im*possibility of existence, that is, as the absolute nothingness of *Da-sein*. Death is not pieced on to *Da-sein* as its 'end,' but, as care, *Da-sein* is the thrown (that is, null) ground of its death. The nothingness primordially dominant in the being of *Da-sein* is revealed to it in authentic being-toward-death. Anticipation makes being-guilty evident only on the basis of the *whole* being of *Da-sein*" (Heidegger, *Being and Time*, 283).

21. Heidegger, *Introduction to Metaphysics*, 6–7.

professed agnosticism to outright atheism. This antireligious progression makes sense if one takes the methodologically central experience of *Angst* to reveal the essential mortality and finitude of *Da-sein*.

A FORK IN THE ROAD AHEAD

A recent commentator states:

> To the end of metaphysics, to the death of God, belongs a historical occurrence [*Ereignis*] that does not stop, or end, and that remains to be thought as it gives itself to be thought. It is this struggle to think in the death or the absence of God and metaphysical meanings that is indicated in the supplementary title to *Contributions*, where Heidegger has already situated the thinking of the book as occurring out of and in this struggle, as a thinking *vom Ereignis*.[22]

There is something decidedly odd about this statement. Far from dead, God—or at least "the god,"[23] "the gods,"[24] "the divinity of the gods,"[25] "the last god,"[26] "the godhood of the other god,"[27] or "the trembling of this divinization"[28]—seems to be alive and well in the pages of the *Beiträge*. What explains the sudden reappearance of religious or quasi-religious discourse in Heidegger's writings from 1938 onward?[29]

22. Vallega, "Being-Historical Thinking," 50.
23. Heidegger, *Contributions to Philosophy*, 207.
24. Heidegger, *Contributions to Philosophy*, 346.
25. Heidegger, *Contributions to Philosophy*, 400.
26. Heidegger, *Contributions to Philosophy*, 206.
27. Heidegger, *Contributions to Philosophy*, 110.
28. Heidegger, *Contributions to Philosophy*, 192.

29. Dennis J. Schmidt writes that "while it is in some sense undeniable that here one finds the development of, if not a theology, something like a 'theological difference,' it is important to understand the ways in which the discussion of the last god is not, in the first instance at least, a theological discussion" (Schmidt, "Strategies for a Possible Reading," 41–42). The present study will argue that if not in the first then at least in the second instance, Heidegger's discussion of the last god and related themes raises a definite theological issue, the successful resolution of which gestures toward a specific version of theology. Schmidt holds that "in *Contributions* we find a contribution to politics" even though "no positive theory or doctrine of political life is proffered" in the *Beiträge* (Schmidt, "Strategies for a Possible Reading," 42). If, as Schmidt, proposes, Heidegger's main political contribution there is to consider the failure of any politics grounded on ethical notions of good and evil, then it remains totally unclear how Heidegger would foster the kind of political cooperation and community that these ethical notions were

Answering this question requires us to think through two possible responses to the fundamental ontological incompatibility between theology and Heideggerian existential phenomenology that has been described. The first possible response takes its cue from Heidegger's Luther-inspired remark in *Sein und Zeit* to the effect that theology must free itself from any distorting conceptual apparatus insufficient for the range of theological problems. Echoing Luther's own hostility to all philosophy of religion, one might go so far as to reject *any* intrusion of philosophy into the discipline of theology. As Heidegger suggests at one point in "Phenomenology and Theology," perhaps there could even be a radically non-conceptual faith in which not only philosophy but also the very idea of theology as a coherent body of doctrine is abandoned.

The second possible response toes the line drawn in the sand by Heidegger's 1920 inaugural lecture "*Was ist Metaphysik?*":

> Holding itself out into the nothing, *Da-sein* is in each case already beyond beings as a whole. This being beyond beings we call "transcendence." If in the ground of its essence *Da-sein* were not transcending, which now means, if it were not in advance holding itself out into the nothing, then it could never be related to beings nor even to itself.[30]

Furthermore,

> Being and the nothing do belong together, not because both—from the point of view of the Hegelian concept of thought—agree in their indeterminateness and immediacy, but rather because being itself is essentially finite and reveals itself only in the transcendence of *Da-sein* which is held out into the nothing.[31]

The goal here is to divest "transcendence" of any religious connotations. Instead, the term should be interpreted in a purely existential and phenomenological manner as the world of transient beings disclosed to *Da-sein*

---

originally intended to underwrite. For additional skepticism about Heidegger's alleged contribution to politics see Dillard, "Review."

30. Heidegger, "What is Metaphysics?," 103.

31. Heidegger, "What is Metaphysics?," 108. In this and the previously quoted passage, I have replaced "*Dasein*" with "*Da-sein*" to ensure terminological consistency. See footnote 12 above and chapter 3 for the different uses of "*Da-sein*" in *Sein und Zeit* and the *Beiträge zur Philosophie*. In the second passage, I have also written "being" instead of "Being" in order to avoid any undue reification of the original German word *Sein*.

within the finite horizon delimited by its own ultimate demise. Phenomenological philosophy is thereby purged of any theological remnants.

The next two chapters will evaluate each of these extreme responses. To anticipate a bit, we will be in a position to understand Heidegger's unexpected return to theologically inflected discourse in the *Beiträge* if (1) theology without philosophy is insufficient for overcoming certain theological problems; (2) philosophy—specifically, *Angst*-driven Heideggerian existential phenomenology—without theology turns out to be an oxymoron because the philosophy in question is encumbered with definite theological commitments; and (3) the philosophical perspective of the *Beiträge* provides sufficient resources for resolving the aforementioned theological problems while allowing the question of the relationship between humanity and divinity to be posed in a whole new light.

Chapter 2

Theology without Philosophy

Human reason with all its wisdom can bring it no further than
to instruct people how to live honestly and decently in the world,
how to keep house, build, etc., things learned from philosophy and
heathenish books. But how they should learn to know God and his
dear Son, Christ Jesus, and to be saved, this alone the Holy Ghost
teaches through God's Word; for philosophy understands naught
of divine matters.[1]

RESUMÉ: UNTYING THE KNOT BY LOSING
A THREAD

We noted how Heidegger's 1927 "Phenomenology and Theology" sets
forth a particular conception of the relation between theology and philosophy. Theology is the ontic science that, through conceptual interpretation,
brings both greater transparency and increasing difficulty to faith in the
crucified God, Jesus Christ. Phenomenological philosophy, by contrast, is
the ontological science that seeks to clarify the nature of being qua being.
Heidegger envisions a kind of commensalism between these two disciplines in which although philosophy does not depend upon theology, theology can benefit from philosophical analysis of ontological concepts (e.g.,
existence) the theologian takes for granted. Provisionally, we have accepted

---

1. Luther, *Table Talk* 48.

Heidegger's 1929 conception as a framework for our own project of developing a theology of *Streit*.

A formidable obstacle confronting our project is the fundamental ontological incompatibility we have identified between theology as self-reflective faith and phenomenological philosophy as conceived by Heidegger in *Sein und Zeit* and related works. Specifically, while both theology and Heideggerian existential phenomenology acknowledge the fact of human existence, they nevertheless propound radically conflicting visions of it. Theology maintains that human existence is created by God and continues forever, since each human being will continue to exist after his or her bodily death either in eternal intimacy or eternal estrangement from God. Heideggerian existential phenomenology takes the unsettling experience of *Angst* or anxiety to reveal human existence as an essentially finite "thrownness" (*Geworfenheit*) that will terminate for each human being with his or her own death. In light of this irreconcilable difference, the theologian and the existential phenomenologist may understandably feel that if either discipline is to advance, then it must do so without the other. The next chapter will investigate the possibility of Heideggerian existential phenomenology without any theology. The current chapter inquires whether progress in theology as self-reflective, increasingly difficult faith is possible without any philosophical "co-direction" or assistance.

Scholars have documented how both St. Paul's Epistles and Martin Luther's theology of the cross (*theologia crucis*) greatly influenced Heidegger during the early and mid-1920s after his formal break with the Catholic Church in 1918.[2] Especially in his commentaries on Galatians and First and Second Thessalonians, Heidegger is impressed by the distinctively Christian sense of time he takes Paul to articulate, according to which the promise of the *parousia* imbues the early Christian community with an intense and watchful expectation of Christ's return not as some indefinite future occurrence but as an eschatological event that could break into human history at any moment. From his study of Luther, Heidegger imbibes a withering skepticism towards any "theology of glory" (*theologia gloriae*) that seeks to fathom divine mystery by means of human speculative reason; on the contrary, God is only revealed to the believer through paradox and the irrationality of the cross.

2. Two seminal studies are Wolfe, *Heidegger's Eschatology*; McGrath, *Early Heidegger and Medieval Philosophy*. For Paul's influence on Heidegger, see Wolfe, 59–65; McGrath, 190–97; for Luther's influence, see Wolfe, 77–80; McGrath, 151–84. Both works contain copious references to the relevant writings by Heidegger.

Our aim in the following two sections is not to present a comprehensive interpretation of Pauline eschatology, Lutheran theology, or Heidegger's engagement with them. Instead, we will chart a possible trajectory of theological thinking that begins with a difficulty left unresolved by Paul's eschatology and proceeds to consider how aspects of Luther's radically non-philosophical *theologia crucis* might be applied to construct an initially promising solution to this eschatological difficulty. The chapter then concludes by indicating the highly problematic character of the resulting theology that refuses to allow any philosophical involvement at all in matters of faith.

Theology and Pauline Eschatology

What Heidegger calls "Christianness pure and simple,"[3] or faithful Christian existence pursued at both the individual and the communal levels, occurred in the early Christian community and continues today. Yet few if any of the first believers were theologians, and the vast majority of contemporary Christians certainly are not. Why might faithful Christian existence need to become theologically self-reflective in the specific way described by Heidegger in "Phenomenology and Theology"? What motivation could there be for such a peculiar sounding discipline, one that renders faithful Christian existence simultaneously more transparent and more difficult through non-metaphysical conceptual interpretation?

According to the younger Heidegger, "the event of the crucifixion places one's entire existence—as a faithful Christian existence, i.e., one bound to the cross—before God" so that one is reborn with Christ: "*faith = rebirth*."[4] Confronted with the startling events of Christ's crucifixion, death, resurrection, and ascension, early Christian existence is characterized by an overwhelming, life-transforming intensity leading to an eager anticipation of Christ's imminent return. But then Christ does not come back soon, or a few years later, or even after decades and centuries have passed. The indefinite postponement of the *parousia* threatens to dampen primitive Christianity's primal intensity. The longer faith must wait, the greater becomes the risk that its essential passion will dissipate and eventually burn out. Time is the enemy of faithful Christian existence.

---

3. Heidegger, "Phenomenology and Theology," 43.
4. Heidegger, "Phenomenology and Theology," 44.

Paul's eschatology, especially as Heidegger interprets it, may be regarded as an effort to sustain the intensity of original Christianness through non-metaphysical theological reflection.[5] A crucial passage is Paul's counsel in 1 Thessalonians:

> Concerning times and seasons, brothers, you have no need for anything to be written to you. For you yourselves know very well that the day of the Lord will come like a thief in the night. When people are saying "Peace and security," then sudden disaster comes upon them, like labor pains upon a pregnant woman, and they will not escape. But you, brothers, are not in darkness, for that day to overtake you like a thief. For all of you are children of the light and children of the day. We are not of the night or of darkness. Therefore, let us not sleep as the rest do, but let us stay alert and sober. (1 Thess 5:1–6)

On Heidegger's reading, Paul theologically reinvigorates faithful Christian existence by introducing a radically new vision of time, not as a series of temporal moments, but as a particular past (Christ's incarnation, ministry, suffering, death, and ascension) giving rise to an ever-shifting present (remaining steadfastly faithful to the Gospel despite trials and persecutions) in light of a definite future (Christ's eventual return). Each individual Christian, as well as the entire Christian community itself, is then called not to engage in idle speculation about the precise day and hour of the *parousia* but rather to work out the specific facticity of what it means to be a Christian in a fluid moment (*Augenblick*) of watchful resolution (*Entschlossenheit*).[6] It is precisely the inscrutability of Christ's promised return ("For you yourselves know very well that the day of the Lord will come like a thief in the night") that supposedly preserves the existential *frisson* of Christian existence.

Unfortunately, the novel view of time that Heidegger detects in the Pauline Epistles by itself does not prevent primitive Christian intensity

---

5. Wolfe aptly describes this kind of approach as the search "for a religiosity marked by aboriginal experience and a theology capable of giving this experience expression from within (rather than imposing upon it a system from without)" (Wolfe, *Heidegger's Eschatology*, 60).

6. "What must count for the Christian is only the now in which the situation in which he actually stands becomes enacted, not the expectation of an event that is to take place at some fixed point in future time" (Heidegger, *Phänomenologie des religiösen Lebens*, 114). For the English translation of this remark, see Heidegger, *Phenomenology of Religious Life*, 104. It is also cited in McGrath, *Early Heidegger and Medieval Philosophy*, 194.

from transforming into gnawing anxiety over the ongoing non-occurrence of the *parousia*. In fact, Paul's view may make matters even worse. An observation by S. J. McGrath suggests why:

> This enactment [of watchful Christian resolution] is simultaneously a running ahead and a recapitulation. And because it is both of these at once, it is the fullness of a moment that is not separate from what went before and what is yet to come, a *now* that is constitutively determined by the already/not yet, a present that is a relation to the future through the past.[7]

The longer the post-resurrection Christ does not return, the more the *now* of Christian existence becomes constitutively determined by an already of unfulfilled expectation. Furthermore, the fear that the same *now* will continue to be constituted by a not yet of unfilled expectation grows greater and greater. The upshot is that the *now* of Christian existence is increasingly determined not by intense excitement in the face of a joyful reunion but by deepening *ennui*, frustration, and disappointment. As Samuel Beckett's Estragon sadly observes, "Nothing happens. Nobody comes, nobody goes. It's awful."[8]

To the question of what God was doing during all the countless ages before He made heaven and earth, St. Augustine famously answers that the question is misguided, since God exists in uncreated eternity where the moments of created time do not pass but are all present: "Your years never come nor go, but our years pass and others come after them, so that they all may come in their turn. Your years are completely present to you all at once, because they are at a permanent standstill."[9] Presumably, Augustine would also say that from God's timeless perspective, the *parousia* is not indefinitely postponed because the created time at which it occurs is present to God along with all other created times. Yet Augustine's view doesn't really help believers awaiting *parousia*, since they are "orphans of time" who remain firmly situated in the temporal flow of years, decades, centuries, and millennia that come and go. In any case, no theologian trying to develop a thoroughly non-metaphysical conceptual interpretation of faith can take for granted the traditional metaphysical distinction between time and eternity.

7. McGrath, *Early Heidegger and Medieval Philosophy*, 194–95.

8. Beckett, *Waiting for Godot*, 43.

9. Augustine, *Confessions* 11.13, 263. For more on Augustine's view of created time in relation to divine eternity, see Sorabji, *Time, Creation, and Eternity*, 233–39.

The burden of trying to maintain the primal intensity of Christian existence in the face of growing anxiety over when or even whether Christ will return without any recourse to metaphysics explains why Heidegger's phenomenology takes a decidedly non-religious turn in *Sein und Zeit*. As Judith Wolfe observes:

> Heidegger is interested primarily in *Befindlichkeit*—a '*gestimmtes Sichbefinden*' or intuitive, situated 'attunement' within and to the world. Heidegger labels this disposition 'eschatological' affliction; yet his etymological understanding of *Befindlichkeit* (influenced by Schleiermacher) as a function precisely of human situatedness *in* a world resists the inclusion of the traditional Christian object of this disposition, namely the anticipated irruption into the world from without of Christ's *parousia*, as a term of analysis. Consequently, the object of eschatological 'care' or 'affliction' is no longer (as for Paul) the dark and death-filled world *inflected by* its intimate 'solicitation' by Christ, but only that world in its transience.[10]

Bluntly put, each individual *Da-sein* is absolutely certain not only that it can die at any moment but also that it eventually *will* die. If its death is the termination of each individual *Da-sein*'s existence, then death can serve as an absolute and non-negotiable object of our *Befindlichkeit* to replace a wavering and unsatisfyingly elusive *parousia*. Fervent hope in Christ's return is thus abandoned in favor of the bracing recognition that we are essentially finite. Quixotic, otherworldly theology is out. Tough-minded, this-worldly existential phenomenology is in.

Or is it? Might there be some other non-metaphysical path forward for a theology grappling with the eschatological conundrum? To sound out this possibility, we turn now to Luther.

Luther on Divine Contrariety

Theses 19 and 20 of Luther's *Heidelberg Disputations* draw a sharp contrast between the theology of glory (*theologia gloriae*) and the theology of the cross (*theologia crucis*):

> 19. That person is not rightly called a theologian who looks upon the invisible things of God as though they were clearly perceptible through things that have actually happened.

10. Wolfe, *Heidegger's Eschatology*, 64.

20. He deserves to be called a theologian, however, who understands the visible and manifest things of God seen through suffering and the Cross.[11]

Why does Luther think that human reason, including philosophy, has little
if anything to teach us about the invisible things of God through reflection
upon perceptible things? His answer is that, as a result of the Fall, human
nature has become totally corrupted by original sin, so that through the
exercise of our reason we can learn nothing about God except the vaguest
generalities: as Luther trenchantly remarks, "Reason [is] entirely corrupt
and altogether changed!"[12]

Interestingly, the Heidegger of the mid-1920s concurs with Luther's
highly pessimistic assessment of our postlapsarian situation: "The being of
man as such is sin. Sin is nothing other than the opposite of faith, where
faith means standing (to be placed) before God. It [sin] is thus not an adherence to the moral nature of man but rather is his actual core."[13] According to Luther, Adam and Eve's first sin consists in their listening to the
tempting serpent's word rather than to the word of God, thereby becoming
drawn into a dispute (*disputatio*) between the two. The result is not merely
damaging but completely destructive: "With it [the first sin], they lose their
original being before God."[14] Their being open to God in the state of innocence is now supplanted by an entirely different kind of being that is
marked by total enmity towards Him. Remarkably, Luther goes so far as to
say that even Adam and Eve's postlapsarian abilities to address and to hear
God derive not from intact human nature itself but solely from extraneous
divine grace. Heidegger agrees:

11. Luther, *Luther's Works*, 166.

12. Luther, *Luther's Works*, 142. "The vaguest generalities" include "the invisible attributes of eternal power and divinity," which St. Paul takes to be been understood and perceived in what God has made since the creation of the world (Rom 1:20). Luther denies
that this minimal natural knowledge suffices to teach us how to relate to God properly,
let alone how to attain salvation. For further discussion of this issue, see McGrath, *Early
Heidegger and Medieval Philosophy*, 158–59.

13. Heidegger, "Das Problem," 31 (my translation). The original German text reads:
"Das Sein des Menschen als solchen selbst ist Sünde. Sünde ist nichts anderes als der
Gegensatz zum Glauben, wobei Glauben heißt: vor Gott stehen (gestellt sein). Sie is also
nicht ein Anhaften der moralischen Beschaffenheit des Menschen, sondern sein eigentli-
cher Kern."

14. "Mit ihr verlieren sie ihre ursprüngliches Sein vor Gott" (Heidegger, "Das Problem," 32).

> And this condition of man is brought about by God, insofar as
> it is wholly by grace that after the Fall he did not remain silent
> but instead speaks. What is still noteworthy is how God's being is
> always grasped as the word and man's fundamental relationship to
> him as hearing.

Both before and after the Fall, God speaks while Adam and Eve hear Him.
Yet in the wake of their sin their and their descendants' ability to hear and
to answer God comes not from human nature but from God alone. The
clear implication is that original sin destroys any natural human capacity to
hear, to answer, and presumably also to discern God through the exercise
of reason.

At first blush, the justification given by Luther and echoed by the
younger Heidegger of why our reason—especially in the form of speculative
philosophy—is incapable of uncovering core truths about divinity is deeply
problematic. Luther boldly claims that the first sins committed by Adam
and Eve totally corrupted human nature and "altogether changed" human
reason. But then it is puzzling why these sins didn't *destroy* originally innocent human nature existing in intuitive openness to God and *replace* it with
something else: after the Fall, there are no longer genuine human beings;
instead, there is a species of thoroughly sinful animals, among whom we
must count ourselves, who bodily resemble genuine human beings yet possess significantly weaker cognitive capacities vis-à-vis God, to the extent
that they cannot even hear or address Him without an extraneous act of
divine grace. Worse, if, as Heidegger says, the very core of our postlapsarian
being is sin, then Christ cannot redeem us by taking away our sin. For if
our being is sin then sin is essential to what we are, so that taking away our
sin would annihilate us no less than taking away its three-sidedness would
annihilate a triangle.[15]

Admittedly, a classical metaphysical theory of human nature along
broadly Aristotelian lines might be advanced in order to explain why the
first sins do not destroy human nature by taking away an essential attribute
but only wound human nature by depriving it of a non-essential attribute.
The loss of primordial innocence and intuitive openness to God would then
constitute an accidental change of human nature into a damaged version of
itself, rather than a substantial change of human nature into some other

15. It is perhaps for this reason that Kierkegaard, speaking through his pseudonym
Vigilius Haufniensis, praises the 1577 Lutheran *Formula of Concord* for proscribing the
view that because of original sin, sin is man's substance. See Kierkegaard, *Concept of
Anxiety*, 34.

kind of creature entirely. Since Luther denies that metaphysics can make any positive contribution to theology, obviously this kind of metaphysical response is not available to him. The response is also not available to anyone else who seeks to resolve the fundamental conflict between theology and philosophy by repudiating *all* philosophy, from classical metaphysics to Heideggerian existential phenomenology.

How might Luther, or someone like the younger Heidegger who is sympathetic to Luther's basic theological stance, counter the foregoing objection without plunging headlong into metaphysics? Luther enunciates a cardinal principle of his *theologia crucis* by contrasting our ordinary concepts of wisdom and power with God's wisdom and power:

> It is clear that these are hidden inside, but more amazingly, that they are hidden under the form of the opposite (*sub contrario suo abscondita sunt*). So whoever totally humiliates himself in the eyes of the world (*coram mundo*) is totally exalted in the sight of God (*coram Deo*).[16]

We may call this *the contrariety principle*. According to it, God's wisdom and power are revealed to us as "hidden under the form of the opposite" or their contraries consisting of foolishness and weakness as we encounter them in our ordinary, everyday world. The focal point of Luther's contrariety principle is the crucifixion of Christ, where God's supreme wisdom and power is revealed to us under the opposite forms of an itinerant preacher who foolishly returns to a city brimming with his enemies and then dies completely helpless at their hands. How might the contrariety principle be applied to the theological problem of original sin now confronting us?

The idea of a human nature that has been totally destroyed by sin and then subsequently redeemed is paradoxical, if not downright absurd: once something has been destroyed, it is hard to see how it can be repaired or redeemed. Paradox or absurdity is an even more extreme opposite of human wisdom, since what is wholly incomprehensible is intellectually much worse than what is merely false or than what is true yet unsubstantiated. Trying to comprehend our current situation in terms of something incomprehensible plunges us into an abyss of cognitive futility and existential helplessness. It is precisely here that Luther's contrariety principle strikes like theological lightning. The Cross reveals that the absolute power and supreme wisdom of divinity are revealed to us as hidden under their opposite

16. Luther, *D. Martin Luthers Werke*, 4:35–37. Translated and quoted in McGrath, *Luther's Theology of the Cross*, 155.

forms of what ordinarily passes for complete weakness and utter folly. If we embrace the full scope of this Christocentric revelation, then we must acknowledge that God's absolute power and supreme wisdom are also revealed as hidden under the contrary forms consisting of our own cognitive helplessness as we grapple with the absurdity of human nature both totally destroyed by sin and somehow subsequently redeemed by grace. Wherever God's absolute power and supreme wisdom are present, no sin whatsoever can be co-present. Thus the presence of absolute divine power and wisdom in the very midst of our own cognitive helplessness liberates us from all sin—original or otherwise—provided that we take to heart what the Cross teaches us about God's mysterious manner of revealing Himself to us. As Luther never tires of reminding us, truly we are saved through faith alone.

On this reading of Luther's *theologia crucis*, the inability of our reason to grasp the invisible things of God is not deduced from a paradoxical doctrine of original sin that teeters on the verge of collapse into absurdity unless it is propped up by some pagan metaphysical theory. On the contrary, the crucifixion teaches us that the paradoxical or even the absurd is the non-negotiable criterion for thinking about all things pertaining to God and our relationship with Him, as opposed to instructing people how to live honestly and decently in the world, how to keep house, how to build, and how to pursue other purely secular matters. Indeed, if we are *not* wrestling with paradox or absurdity, then we are not really thinking about God but instead about something else.[17] By wrongly identifying God with what is not God, a theology of glory succumbs to idolatry. The Lutheran emphasis on matters of faith as unavoidably paradoxical, obscure, and enigmatic is also congenial to the possibility of a *Streit* theology described in the first chapter, both in its repudiation of metaphysics as well as in its insistence that our ongoing struggle to wrest disclosure and clarity from hiddenness and obscurity is our quintessential experience of the holy.

17. This point has a direct bearing on the Calvinistic doctrine of original sin, according to which God imputes guilt for Adam's sin to all of Adam's descendants. Either such imputation is free from any paradox or it is not. If imputation of guilt is free from paradox, then by Luther's contrariety principle it has nothing whatsoever to with our sinful relationship to God. If, however, imputation of guilt is paradoxical (since it appears no less absurd for a just God to impute guilt for Adam's sin to Adam's descendants who didn't even exist when Adam sinned), then the Calvinistic paradox of imputed guilt is no real theological advance over the original Lutheran paradox of human nature totally corrupted by original sin yet subsequently redeemed. We would do better simply to stick with the latter and work through the theological consequences of Luther's contrariety principle.

This impression is confirmed by some of Heidegger's writings dating from the 1930s. There, Heidegger's description of the tension between unconcealment ("world") and concealment ("earth") within the overall event of truth strongly resonates with Luther's stress on how divine attributes are revealed as hidden under their contrary forms. The parallel is especially apparent in Heidegger's description of how an ancient Greek temple *in situ* opens up a specific world of warriors, heroes, priests, and slaves while simultaneously setting this world back on its indigenous ground that includes the native rock from which the temple is created:

> That into which the work sets itself back and which causes it to come forth in this setting back we called the earth. Earth is that which comes forth and shelters. Earth, self-dependent, is effortless and untiring. Upon the earth and in it, historical man grounds his dwelling in the world. In setting up a world, the work sets forth the earth. This setting forth must be thought here in the strict sense of the word. The work moves the earth itself into the Open of a world and keeps it there. *The work lets the earth be an earth.*[18]

As Heidegger elaborates, the autochthonous earth set forth by the temple-work does not become disclosed in terms of its exact weight, the wavelengths of its colors, or other purely quantitative properties but instead "shows itself only when it remains undisclosed and unexplained" because "The earth is essentially self-secluding. To set forth the earth means to bring it into the Open as the self-secluding."[19] The Heideggerian dialectic between "earth" paradoxically revealed through seclusion within the disclosing event of "world" is strongly reminiscent of the Lutheran dialectic between God's power and wisdom paradoxically revealed through hiddenness under their contrary forms in the disclosing event of the crucifixion.

In a speculative vein, let us now consider how Luther's contrariety principle might be used to construct a wholly non-metaphysical, purely theological solution to the previously noted problem with Paul's eschatology. Recall that during the indefinitely prolonged absence of the risen Christ's return at the *parousia*, the condition or *Befindlichkeit* of individual and collective Christian existence is one of eschatological affliction, an increasingly crippling anxiety stoked by ignorance of precisely when or even whether Jesus will ever return. By Luther's contrariety principle, meditation on Jesus's crucifixion teaches us that God's power and wisdom, and hence

18. Heidegger, "Origin of the Work of Art," 46.

19. Heidegger, "Origin of the Work of Art," 47.

God himself, are revealed and made present to us as hidden under the opposite forms of what is ordinary regarded as weakness and foolishness. Thus the contrariety principle serves as a legend or key that enables us to detect the divine presence hidden in the map of various afflictive situations. For example, in the afflictive situation where we experience cognitive futility and existential helplessness when we are confronted with the flagrant absurdity of a human nature that is both destroyed by sin and subsequently redeemed by Christ, the presence of God's power and wisdom under these contrary forms liberates us from sin, so long as we faithfully take to heart the theological lesson of the crucifixion.

In the different situation of eschatological affliction, the contrariety principle again directs us to detect the presence of divine power and wisdom hidden under the contrary forms of our anxiously awaiting Christ's return while remaining ignorant of when or whether it will occur. However—and here we come to a crucial point in our speculations—we are now faithful Christians who have already been liberated from sin through the presence of divine power and wisdom hidden under the contrary forms of our cognitive futility and existential helplessness. Thus God's hidden presence in the situation of eschatological affliction must be of a new kind. Specifically, hidden under the contrary forms of our rising anxiety and numbing ignorance is the presence of God incarnate in the risen Christ. Christ's *parousia* is not a protracted absence, some hazy future moment that has not yet become actual, but a protracted happening or event (as the later Heidegger might say, an *Ereignis*) beginning with the early Christians' anxious waiting for the risen Christ, continuing through contemporary Christians' ever more agonized waiting for him, and culminating in the awesome transparency of our ultimate realization that the risen Christ has already been with all of us all along the way. We are not called to eschew but rather to embrace our eschatological anxiety and ignorance as the contrary and intensifying forms under which the risen Christ is increasingly revealed to us.

A TRIPLE THREAT

We have been exploring the possibility of circumventing the fundamental incompatibility between theology and Heideggerian existential phenomenology by rejecting any metaphysical or other philosophical involvement in the project of providing a conceptual interpretation that makes self-reflective faith both more transparent and more difficult. Speculations guided by the contrariety principle at the heart of Luther's *theologica crucis* have lead us to a geography of holy enigma in which the phenomenological data of human suffering, helplessness, ignorance, and anxiety in the face of paradox or absurdity are non-negotiable criteria for our recognizing the presence of divinity hidden under these contrary forms. Is this the version of broadly Heideggerian *Streit* theology we seek? For three reasons, the answer must be "No."

The first reason is psychological. According to the view under consideration, anxiety, frustration, bewilderment, helplessness, and other painful feelings aroused by uncertainty, paradox, or absurdity indicate the various ways in which divine power and wisdom are at work yet hidden under these contrary forms. Negative affectivity seems to be a permanent feature of our relationship with God. The worry is that a conceptual interpretation of faith that makes faith increasingly difficult eventually will make faith *too* difficult so that people simply stop believing altogether. We are merely human, and as human we can only tolerate a limited amount of unpleasant experience. To be sure, there will always be mysteries about God we cannot understand. But it would be highly paradoxical indeed, if not complete lunacy, to envision our endless dwelling with God in heaven as marked by our endless *distress* over whatever it is about Him we still cannot grasp. If heaven is not to become an unbearable hell for us, then at least there our ignorance must somehow also be bliss.

The second reason is more philosophical. In the course of his debate with Erasmus over free will, Luther accuses his opponent of contradicting himself:

> You plainly assert that the will is effective in things pertaining to eternal salvation, when you speak of its striving. And again you assert that it is passive, when you say that without the mercy of God it is ineffective. But you fail to define the limits within which we should think of the will as acting and as being acted upon. Thus you keep us in ignorance as to how far the mercy of God extends, and how far our own will extends; what man's will and God's mercy really *do* effect. That prudence of yours carries you along. You side with neither party and escape safely through Scylla and Charybdis, in order that you may come into open sea, overwhelmed and confounded by the waves, you can then assert all that you now deny, and deny all that you now assert![20]

20. Luther, "Bondage of the Will," 105.

43

The substance of Luther's charge is that since Erasmus fails to delimit the respective contributions of human striving and divine grace to a person's receiving eternal salvation, he winds up asserting the very thing he denies—namely, that someone both is and is not saved solely through the exercise of her own free will without any assistance from divine grace.

From the perspective of the theological extremism we have been charting in the present chapter, Erasmus has an easy retort. Suppose he is contradicting himself. So what? God is present to us hidden in the baffling paradox that a person is saved solely by the exercise of her own free will as well as solely through the operation of divine grace. Better yet, God is present to us hidden in the unnerving absurdity that a person both is and is not entirely saved by her own free will, as well as in the mind-numbing contradiction that she both is and is not entirely saved through the operation of divine grace. After all, bafflement and consternation in the face of paradox, absurdity, or contradiction are all contrary forms under which God in His power and wisdom is made present to us. The *Streit* theologian cannot consistently make our struggle with irresolvable paradox, absurdity, or contradiction definitive of our relationship with God while at the same time rejecting other views on the ground that they plunge us into irresolvable paradox, absurdity, or contradiction. Unless a principled distinction between acceptable and unacceptable paradoxes can be drawn, paradox must be eradicated as much possible from our theological thinking. Either way, additional philosophical resources are needed in order to make any headway here.

The third reason for declining the option of a *Streit* theology without any philosophy is, surprisingly, theological. At another point in his debate with Erasmus, Luther writes:

> God in His own nature and majesty is to be left alone. In this respect we have nothing to do with Him, nor does He wish us to deal with Him. We have to deal with Him as clothed in as delivered to us by His word. God Preached deplores the death which He finds in His people, which He desires to remove from them. But God Hidden in majesty neither deplores, nor takes away death, but works life and death and all things; nor is He kept bound to His word, but has kept Himself free over all things.[21]

---

21. Luther, "Bondage of the Will," 126.

Luther goes so far as to claim that "God does not will the death of a sinner in *His Word*—but He does it by that inscrutable will."[22] Thus what God in His incarnate and revealed Word (*Deus incarnates et relevatus*) wills (e.g., that no sinner is predestined to damnation) contradicts what God in His hidden majesty (*Deus absconditus*) wills (e.g., that some sinners are predestined to damnation).

The result runs the risk of pulling the rug out from under the entire speculative edifice that has been erected so far. Previously, faithful Christians were assured of Christ's redeeming presence revealed to them under the contrary forms of their own cognitive futility and existential helplessness before the paradox of original sin. Subsequently, Christ's unfolding presence in the *parousia* was disclosed to them under the contrary forms of their anxious waiting in eschatological ignorance. Now confronted with the even more bracing contradiction between *Deus incarnates et revelatus* and *Deus absconditus*, the faithful are saddled with the truly anguishing prospect of God taking back with His hidden hand what He had presumably given with His revealed hand: perhaps through God's hidden fiat, Christ's redeeming wisdom and power were never really present under the contrary forms of cognitive futility and existential helplessness! Once that support is gone, there is no guarantee that a different mode of Christ's presence is unfolding under the contrary forms associated with eschatological ignorance. Even if God is somehow present to us in the new situation of predestination affliction under the contrary form of our anguish before the paradox of the revealed versus the hidden God, who can say with certainty that His presence is one of redeeming love rather than damning hatred?[23] The whole house of cards comes tumbling down.

One might try to block this unpalatable consequence by driving a wedge between Luther's earlier *theologia crucis* and Luther's later theology of the *Deus absconditus*:

> The *Deus incarnatus* must find himself reduced to tears as he sees the *Deus absonditus* consigning men to perdition.[24] Not only do such statements suggest that Luther has abandoned his earlier principle of deriving theology solely on the basis of the cross: they

---

22. Luther, *D. Martin Luthers Werke*, 18:28–29, quoted in McGrath, *Luther's Theology of the Cross*, 166.

23. Perhaps, as the character Karin in Ingmar Bergman's film *Through a Glass Darkly* says, the God behind the wall is a spider with a stony face and eyes that are cold and calm.

24. Paraphrased from Luther, *D. Martin Luthers Werke*, 18:32–33.

also suggest that the cross is not the final word of God on anything. While we cannot pursue the origins of this second understanding of the *Deus absconditus*, it seems to us that is not a necessary consequence of the first, discussed above.[25]

Setting aside the question of whether some such reply is available to Luther himself, it will not work for the Luther-inspired, paradox-laden version of theology without philosophy that we have been considering. If theology's goal is to make self-reflective faith not easier but even more difficult, then anguishing over the contradiction of a God who both does and does not predestine some sinners to eternal damnation reveals divine wisdom and power under a contrary form that is more alien to human understanding than anything so far. Given the conception of theology Heidegger sketches in "Phenomenology and Theology," *theologia Deus absconditus* does not depart from but deepens *theologia crucis*.

On a more positive note, we have learned a few things that should help to guide our forthcoming analyses. Pursuing a non-metaphysical theology of *Streit* within Heidegger's 1927 framework will require at least some philosophical "co-direction." If a particular philosophy contains resources we can use to craft non-metaphysical solutions to the eschatological and harmatiological paradoxes we have encountered in St. Paul and Luther, then we have a strong *prima facie* reason to think that the philosophy in question is suitable for our project of developing a Heideggerian theology of *Streit*. Treating the phenomenon of Christ's crucifixion as a kind of legend or key to a map of various other situations is also an intriguing idea to which we will return to it in a later chapter. First, though, we must reckon with the other extreme response to the fundamental incompatibility between theology and Heideggerian existential phenomenology that abandons the former in favor of the latter.

25. McGrath, *Luther's Theology of the Cross*, 166.

Chapter 3

Philosophy without Theology

Anxiety can be compared with dizziness. He whose eye happens to look down into the yawning abyss becomes dizzy. But what is the reason? It is just as much his own eye as the abyss, for suppose he had not looked down. It is in this way that anxiety is the dizziness of freedom that emerges when spirit wants to posit the synthesis, and freedom now looks down into its own possibility and then grabs hold of finiteness to support itself. In this dizziness freedom subsides.[1]

ANXIETY AGAIN

ACCORDING TO KIERKEGAARD, ANXIETY is the dizzying experience I have when I teeter at the edge of an abyss. The abyss is the paradox of Christ, who somehow embodies "the infinite qualitative difference between God and man."[2] My experience is dizzying because I and I alone am somehow responsible for freely deciding either to dismiss this paradox as outrageously offensive and so to dissipate my freedom in the myriad resources of my own finitude, or instead to embrace the paradox in faithful worship that "posits the synthesis" by defining myself as a genuine Christian for all eternity.[3]

1. Kierkegaard, *Concept of Anxiety*, 75.

2. Kierkegaard, *Concept of Anxiety*, 127.

3. "The person who does not take offense *worships* in faith. But to worship, which is the expression of faith, is to express that the infinite, chasmic, qualitative abyss between

Thus on Kierkegaard's view, the experience of anxiety is a form of religious intentionality. What anxiety is purportedly "about"—i.e., what it supposedly reveals to the subject experiencing it—is the uncanny unity of humanity with divinity in Christ. The subject must then either choose to reject the purported intentional correlate of anxiety as outrageous, false, perhaps even as nonsensical, or to accept it as life-transforming truth. Yet as we have seen, anxiety has also been viewed in avowedly non-religious terms. Such is the case with Heidegger's existential phenomenology in *Sein und Zeit*: what anxiety is "about" or discloses to *Da-sein* is the uncanny fact that all of its ongoing possibilities and projects will ultimately terminate in its own death as "the possibility of the absolute impossibility of *Da-sein*"[4] which *Da-sein* may then evade by either by losing itself in inauthenticity of *das Man* or embrace through the resolute authenticity of *Entschlossenheit*. This non-religious construal of anxiety is essential to Heidegger's *Sein und Zeit* analysis of *Da-sein*, since anxiety makes available to *Da-sein* the essentially finite entirety of its own individualized being as a theme for further phenomenological description.

If philosophy is taken to encompass Heidegger's non-religious existential phenomenology, then a second extreme response to the conflicting views of human existence set forth by theology and philosophy becomes possible. Simply put, one might repudiate theology along with its faith-based view of human existence as something that does not terminate with bodily death in favor of Heideggerian existential phenomenological analysis aimed at elucidating the manifold structures of human being as well as the nature of being in general.

The goal of the current chapter is to determine whether Heidegger's existential phenomenology guided by the experience of anxiety in the face of the uncanny is free from any religious commitments or the need to take religious issues seriously. A possible theological criticism is that Heidegger injects substantive religious content into his phenomenology by using terms traditionally associated with religious notions of sin and guilt. Simply

---

them [humanity and divinity] is confirmed" (Kierkegaard, *Sickness Unto Death*, 129). "But for an individual to be formed absolutely and infinitely by possibility, that individual must be honest toward possibility and have faith" (Kierkegaard, *Concept of Anxiety*, 189).

4. Heidegger, *Being and Time*, 232. For the disclosure of *Da-sein's* uncanny individuation through the experience of anxiety, see Heidegger, *Being and Time*, 272: "Understanding the call discloses one's own *Da-sein* in the uncanniness of its individuation. The uncanniness revealed in understanding is genuinely disclosed by the attunement of *Angst* belonging to it."

disavowing these connotations comes across as dogmatic and unconvincing. A more nuanced theological criticism is that Heidegger's phenomenology essentially depends on *Da-sein*'s desire to transcend itself, where the self-transcendence in question must be religiously conceived as *Da-sein*'s ultimate union with God. The first two sections argue that these challenges to the alleged religious neutrality of Heidegger's philosophy, though suggestive, do not succeed.

The final two sections then develop an internal theological critique that draws upon the very resources of Heidegger's own *Angst*-driven phenomenology from 1929 onward. Briefly, the elasticity of anxiety in the face of the uncanny belies Heidegger's contention that the proper intentional correlate of *Angst* is essentially finite human existence, rather than something uncanny that is distinct from *Da-sein*, any other particular being, the totality of beings, being itself, or absolute nothingness. A clue from St. Bonaventure will help to drive the point home without encumbering the critique with excessive metaphysical baggage. Once we have set aside the extreme options of theology without philosophy or philosophy without theology, we will be in a better position to look for philosophical tools that prove useful in constructing a non-metaphysical *Streit* theology within Heidegger's "Phenomenology and Theology" framework.

Religious Assumption or Dogmatic Presumption?

Throughout *Sein und Zeit*, Heidegger uses terms like "guilt" (*Schuld*) or "guilty" (*schuldig*), "falling prey" (*Verfallen*), and "call of conscience" (*Gewissenruf, Ruf des Gewissens*), all of which carry strong religious connotations. Despite Heidegger's insistence that phenomenology, unlike theology, is an ontically neutral science of phenomena or "beings as they show themselves in themselves"[5] and further that his ontology guided by "the being guilty that belongs primordially to the constitution of the being of *Da-sein*" knows "nothing about sin in principle,"[6] it is natural to wonder whether Heidegger is smuggling in tacit religious content.

S. J. McGrath answers forcefully in the affirmative:

> Heidegger's "methodological atheism," if intended as an effort to think being free of religious assumption, fails from the beginning:

5. Heidegger, *Being and Time*, 30–31.
6. Heidegger, *Being and Time*, 410–11.

far from thinking independently of his religious context, Heidegger works with ideas that, according to his own study of Christianity, depend upon their original religious context.[7]

Either the terms in question are either being used in a manner that still depends on their original religious context or they are not. If so, then Heidegger's existential phenomenology is religiously loaded; if not, then in Heidegger's hands the terms have become empty ciphers stripped of any definite significance.

Heidegger might counter that from a purely phenomenological standpoint, religious ideas of sin, guilt, and so forth have no real content because the spiritual conditions they purport to describe are not directly given to us in experience. So far as he can make any sense out of the associated terminology, it is only in connection with the experientially salient structures of *Da-sein* uncovered by his own phenomenological investigations. For example, the only sense that Heidegger can assign to "guilt" is the experiential fact that *Da-sein* finds itself "thrown" into the world at a particular place and time (e.g., Germany during the early twentieth century) under specific conditions (being raised as a male near the Black Forest) it did not choose.[8]

A comparison with a similar issue in the very different context of W. V. Quine's philosophy is instructive. Quine defines the *stimulus meaning* of a sentence S for a speaker as the ordered pair consisting the set of all and only sensory stimuli that would prompt the speaker's assent to S when queried (S's affirmative stimulus meaning) and the set of all and only sensory stimuli that would prompt S's dissent from S when queried (S's negative stimulus meaning).[9] To the extent that Quine can make any sense out of the term "the meaning of S," it is only with his ersatz-behaviorist notion of S's stimulus meaning that has nothing to do with any traditional semantic notions. Hence in saying that a sentence has (stimulus) meaning, Quine is definitely *not* claiming that the sentence expresses a medieval signification, a mental content or a Fregean sense (*Sinn*). Similarly, Heidegger dissociates "guilt," "falling," and related terms from their traditional religious connotations in favor of his own ersatz phenomenological concepts. Thus when he

7. McGrath, *Heidegger*, 112–13.

8. See Heidegger, *Being and Time*, 261–62, where *Da-sein*'s being "guilty" is described as follows: "*Da-sein* exists as thrown, brought into its there *not* of its own accord. It exists as a potentiality-of-being which belongs to itself, and yet has *not* given itself to itself. Existing, it never gets back behind its thrownness so that it could expressly release its 'that-it-is-and-has-to-be' from its *being* a self and lead it into the there."

9. See Quine, *Word and Object*, 32–33.

says, for instance, that *Da-sein* is guilty or fallen, Heidegger is definitely *not* claiming that *Da-sein* is fallen in sin before God, but merely that *Da-sein* does not have complete control over how it comes to exist in a world.

Still, one might persist, unlike Quine, who argues extensively against traditional semantic notions like synonymy and analyticity, Heidegger flatly rejects without giving any supporting argument the Christian ideas of guilt and falling in favor of a radically non-Christian interpretation of human existence as finite and Godforsaken. In doing so, Heidegger violates his own self-imposed stricture to remain ontically neutral. Again, McGrath offers perceptive commentary:

> This edict forbidding ethical-religious commitment is repeated in *Sein und Zeit* as the stipulation that *Da-sein* is not to be inter-preted in terms of any particular mode of being but in terms of its "average everdayness." Yet in the analysis of being-unto-death, the neutral territory of average everydayness is left behind, and one extreme ontic possibility for being-in-*the-world is consulted for a clue as to how ontology can "grasp" Da-sein* as a whole.[10]

Where is Heidegger's justification for the tendentious presumption that *Da-sein* is only a thrown and finite being-toward-death, as opposed to an accountable and eternal being-before-God?[11] It is nowhere made explicit in *Sein und Zeit*. Rather than religious neutrality, what we seem to encounter there is unwarranted anti-religious bias.

However, a reply based on the nature of phenomenological method itself is available to Heidegger. As Husserl proclaims, the cardinal maxim of phenomenology is "To the things themselves!"[12] Heidegger echoes his former mentor with the observation that "the meaning of the expression 'phenomenon' is established as *what shows itself in itself,* what is manifest."[13] Thus a hallmark of the phenomenological method Heidegger pursues in *Sein und Zeit* is to describe only those things that are shown or manifest to us in our everyday experience. Such things certainly include my own life,

---

10. McGrath, *Early Heidegger and Medieval Philosophy*, 176. McGrath's use of "Das-ein" has been changed to the italicized "*Da-sein*" in order to ensure consistency of usage.

11. McGrath introduces and discusses the notion of human existence as being-before-God in McGrath, *Early Heidegger and Medieval Philosophy*, 243–55.

12. Husserl, *Cartesian Meditations*, 12–13.

13. Heidegger, *Being and Time*, 25. Don Idhe quotes both of these seminal texts from Husserl and Heidegger in Idhe, *Experimental Phenomenology*, 15.

the deaths of others,[14] as well as the anticipation of my own death. God, as well as my life or anyone else's life continuing beyond bodily death, are all definitely *not* things shown or manifest in everyday experience.

Heidegger makes just this point in the following passage:

> If death is defined as the "end" of *Da-sein*, that is, of being-in-the-world, no ontic decision has been made as to whether "after death" another being is still possible, either higher or lower, whether *Da-sein* "lives on" or even, outliving itself, is "immortal." Nor is anything decided ontically about the "otherworldly" and its possibility any more than about the "this-worldly." But our analysis of death remains purely "this-wordly" in that it interprets the phenomenon solely with respect to the question of how it *enters into* actual *Da-sein* in its possibility-of-being. We cannot even *ask* with any methodological assurance about what "*is after death*" until death is understood in its full ontological essence.[15]

Da-sein only experiences itself as a kind of being-in-the-world absorbed in various projects limited by death as something it has witnessed in others and so anticipates for itself. Methodologically, then, Heidegger the existential phenomenologist seems warranted in restricting his attention to a "this-worldly" interpretation of *Da-sein* without deciding either for or against the possibility of life after death. As Judith Wolfe observes, Heidegger "attempts a more radical ontological/phenomenological account of anxiety which does not appeal to extraneous postulates such as eternity or God, but reveals the structural 'self-sufficiency' of factic life."[16]

Essential Dependency?

A subtler theological criticism of Heidegger's existential phenomenology zeroes in on presuppositions underlying his terminology that appears to gesture toward a distinctively religious commitment. Wolfe notes how Heidegger imbues his analysis of *Da-sein* as finite being-in-the-world with a kind of pathos that arises from *Da-sein*'s desire to transcend its own finitude:

---

14. For Heidegger's discussion of our experiencing the death of others, see *Being and Time*, 221–24.

15. Heidegger, *Being and Time*, 230.

16. Wolfe, *Heidegger's Eschatology*, 88.

But while Heidegger's analysis is a virtuoso *plaidoyer* for the ineluctable finitude of human existence, its pathos depends on the assumption of a desire to transcend finitude which the analysis itself cannot and does not attempt to account for. The passionate acts of "shattering oneself against death" or bearing its "affliction" which characterize authentic human existence are predicated on a contrary longing which is as consistently assumed as it is obfuscated by Heidegger's analysis.[17]

Da-sein finds itself in the peculiar predicament of deeply longing to do something it cannot do—namely, to escape the confines of its own finitude. Nevertheless, *Da-sein*'s desire for this impossibility stubbornly persists; only then can *Da-sein* arouse feelings of pity or sympathy as it heroically struggles and suffers in the face of its own unavoidable finitude. Oddly, Heidegger says nothing further about *Da-sein*'s desire to transcend itself.

Following Heidegger's former pupil Edith Stein, Wolff then identifies *Da-sein*'s pathos-laden desire for self-transcendence with love that finds satisfaction only in always having been already loved by a divine and eternal Other:

In other words, authentic resolution (of the kind that grasps its own historicity) is only possible when motivated by love. But loving is only possible if one is already loved, and it is this "already" which is revealed and received in faith. What is more, it is only from this standpoint of knowing oneself to have always already been loved by God that one is capable of seeing natural existence (the "world" of Bultmann's earlier article) as always already graced, "*as creation.*"[18]

The result is pathos, but pathos with a silver lining. *Da-sein* intensely desires to bring about the fact that God has always already loved it. That is not something *Da-sein* by itself can determine; otherwise, a creature would determine something about God, and hence "God" would not really be God. On the other hand, if God Himself *has* in fact always already loved *Da-sein*, then *Da-sein* gets what it wants (God's eternal love)—if not exactly in the way *Da-sein* wants it (initiated by itself rather than initiated by God).

On Wolfe's reading, what makes *Da-sein* worthy of pathos is the impossibility of its deep-seated desire to transcend its own finitude. Yet must

---

17. Wolfe, *Heidegger's Eschatology*, 133.

18. Wolfe, *Heidegger's Eschatology*, 148. The "earlier article" to which Wolfe alludes is Bultmann, "Die Eschatologie des Johannes-Evangeliums."

this impossibility be interpreted in religious terms? In his explanation of the two senses in which *Da-sein* is a "nullity," Heidegger gives a thoroughly non-religious explanation for why *Da-sein*'s desire to transcend its thrown finitude is impossible.[19] He describes the first sense in the following passage:

> Existing, *Da-sein* is its ground, that is, in such a way that it understands itself in terms of possibilities and, thus understanding itself, is thrown being. But this means that, as a potentiality-of-being, it always stands in one possibility or another; it is constantly *not* other possibilities and has relinquished them in its existentiall project.[20]

Da-sein's pursuit of a particular project necessarily precludes it from pursuing certain other projects. My project of devoting years of my life to becoming a neurosurgeon precludes my devoting years of my life to becoming a world-class ballet dancer. Even if I had sufficient talent to pursue both endeavors, limitations of time, stamina, and other circumstances prevent me from doing both in the course of a single lifetime. These practical limitations have nothing to do with any religious commitment.

Wolfe might counter that, strictly speaking, desiring to pursue practically incompatible life-projects is not a desire for something impossible. We can imagine the logical possibility in which *Da-sein* possesses ample talent, time, stamina, and favorable circumstances to pursue any life-projects it wishes to pursue, not simultaneously, but in succession. *Da-sein* would not last forever, but it would last long enough eventually to accomplish whatever it wants to achieve. For *Da-sein*'s predicament to be one of genuine pathos, *Da-sein* must deeply desire to go beyond its thrown condition in a manner that *Da-sein* in principle cannot achieve. Wanting always to have been already been loved by God is definitely a desire that *Da-sein* alone cannot fulfill. Such a desire is obviously framed in explicitly religious terms.

In the concept of existential guilt, we have already encountered the other sense in which Heidegger takes *Da-sein* to be a nullity—namely, the fact that *Da-sein* cannot, so to speak, get behind itself by autonomously determining every facet of its own thrown being-in-the-world:

> Being the ground, that is, existing as thrown, *Da-sein* constantly lags behind its possibilities. It is never existent *before* its ground, but only *from it* and *as it*. Thus being the ground means *never* to

19. For further discussion of the two senses in which Heidegger's takes *Da-sein* to be a nullity, see Dreyfus, *Being-in-the-World*, 306–7.

20. Heidegger, *Being and Time*, 262–63.

gain power over one's own-most being from the ground up. This *not* belongs to the existential meaning of thrownness.[21]

The desire to determine every aspect of its own existence from the ground up is certainly something that *Da-sein* cannot fulfill. In order to determine anything, *Da-sein* must already have some existence. Hence in order to determine its entire existence from the ground up, *Da-sein* would already have to have some existence before it has any existence, which is impossible. Since this desire for something impossible has nothing to do with God but solely with *Da-sein*'s wish to gain total power over its entire being, Heidegger can meet Wolfe's criticism by explaining why *Da-sein* is worthy of *pathos* without appealing to any religious commitment: *Da-sein* heroically struggles and suffers in face of its being unable to determine its own being from the ground up.

Finally, stepping back from the details of Heidegger's *Sein und Zeit* analysis of existential nullity, the pathos of *Da-sein*'s desire for self-transcendence could be given a different non-religious explanation. My desire to transcend the limitations of my own thrown being-in-the-world might consist in my yearning that other human beings thrown into the same world fully reciprocate my love for them, culminating in widespread human solidarity in the face of collective tragedy or catastrophe.[22] I alone cannot fulfill this particular desire to transcend my own finitude, since by myself I cannot determine that other human beings love me to the same extent as I love them. Of course, it may turn out that other human beings do in fact reciprocate my love for them, in which case I get what I want though not exactly in the way I want it. Nevertheless, so far the desire in question is a purely secular one with no reference to religious matters. If we are going to mount a successful challenge to the possibility of Heideggerian existential phenomenology without theology, then we must dig deeper.

THE ELASTICITY OF ANGST

We have seen that for Heidegger, anxiety is an experience possessing intentionality, since anxiety supposedly reveals *something uncanny* to *Dasein*. This uncanny something is the intentional correlate of anxiety, what anxiety purports to be about. According to Heidegger in *Sein und Zeit*, the

---

21. Heidegger, *Being and Time*, 262.

22. This kind of human solidarity is vividly depicted in Camus, *Plague*.

intentional correlate of anxiety is *Da-sein*'s essential finitude, the uncanny fact that *Da-sein*'s thrown being-in-the-world along with its various projects and possibilities will inevitably terminate in *Da-sein*'s individual death. However, when we expand our horizon beyond *Sein und Zeit* to some of Heidegger's works from 1929, the 1930s, and even later, surprisingly we find that what purports to be the uncanny intentional correlate of anxiety is quite different depending on the work in question.

Consider the following passage from a series of lecture Heidegger delivered in 1935 at the University of Freiburg and published later as *Einführung in die Metaphysik*:

> Why is the essent torn away from the possibility of nonbeing? Why does it not simply keep falling back into nonbeing? Now the essent is no longer that which just happens to be present; it begins to waver and oscillate, regardless of whether we recognize the essent in all certainty, regardless of whether we apprehend it in its full scope. Henceforth the essent as such oscillates, insofar as we draw it into question.[23]

"The essent" is Mannheim's translation of Heidegger's original German term *die Seienden*. It designates the totality of all beings, or beings as a whole. Heidegger clams that when we call beings as a whole into question, we experience them as wavering or oscillating in an uncanny way between being and non-being. This ontological vertigo is phenomenologically indistinguishable from *Da-sein*'s anxious dizziness before the prospect of its own uncanny existence that Heidegger appropriates from Kierkegaard and subsequently adapts to his own purposes in *Sein und Zeit*; only now, the intentional correlate of anxiety is not *Da-sein*'s uncanny individual existence but the uncanny contingency of the totality of beings, including yet not restricted to *Da-sein*.

Anxiety in the face of something uncanny also crops up in *Beiträge zur Philosophie (Vom Ereignis)*, a work composed by Heidegger in the period between 1936 and 1938 that was not published during his lifetime. Of particular interest is what Heidegger says concerning the relation between *Da-sein* and *Ereignis* or *beyng*, where the latter does not apply to any particular being or even for beings as a whole but to being itself insofar as it is understood non-metaphysically as the event of appropriation:

---

23. Heidegger, *Introduction to Metaphysics*, 28.

> The opening up of the essential occurrence of *beyng* manifests that *Da-sein* does not accomplish anything, except for catching on to the oscillation of appropriation, i.e., entering into this oscillation and thus for the first time becoming itself: the preserve of the thrown projection, *the grounded one that grounds the ground.*[24]

Heidegger then proceeds to the describe the oscillation of non-metaphysical *beyng* before *Da-sein* even more strikingly as a kind of trembling:

> The trembling of this coming to be of the oscillation in the turning of the event is the most concealed essence of beyng. This concealment is cleared as concealment only in the deepest clearing of the site of the moment. In order to occur essentially in this seldomness and uniqueness, being "needs" *Da-sein*, and *Da-sein* grounds being human, is its ground, insofar as human being in withstanding *Da-sein* grounds *Da-sein* through steadfastness.[25]

This oscillation and trembling are strongly reminiscent of the vertigo and dizziness that, noetically speaking, are characteristic of the experience of anxiety.[26] Yet according to Heidegger in the *Beiträge*, the apparent intentional correlate or *noema* of the oscillation and trembling is neither *Da-sein* itself or the totality of beings as such but non-metaphysical being: *beyng* as the event of appropriation sheltered in beings.[27]

Jumping back to 1929, in Heidegger's inaugural lecture "Was ist die Metaphysik?" at the University of Freiburg, anxiety is there assigned an entirely different uncanny intentional correlate:

> In anxiety, we say, "one feels at ease [*es ist einem unheimlich*]." What is "it" that makes "one" feel at ease? We cannot say what it is before which one feels ill at ease. As a whole it is so for one. All things and we ourselves sink into indifference. This, however, not

---

24. Heidegger, *Contributions to Philosophy*, 188–89. As with *"Da-sein*," all instances of *"beyng"* have been italicized to mark Heidegger's use of it as a technical term.

25. Heidegger, *Contributions to Philosophy*, 206.

26. Though in chapter 6 and (especially) 8, oscillation trembling can begin to emerge as a more positive experience in contrast to the negativity of anxiety.

27. The terms *"noesis"* and *"noema*," along with their cognates, are employed by Husserl to indicate, respectively, the various psychological and affective states associated with a particular experience—the experience's subjective pole, so to speak—and what might be called its objective pole, or that toward which the experience is purportedly directed. For an informative overview of the *noesis-noema* distinction, along with pertinent references to Husserl's writings, see Idhe, *Experimental Phenomenology*, 25–31. We will return to the distinction at the beginning of chapter 4.

in the sense of disappearance. Rather, in this very receding things turn toward us. The receding of beings as a whole that closes in on us in anxiety oppresses us. We can get no hold on things. In the slipping away of beings only this "no hold on things" comes over us and remains. Anxiety reveals the nothing.[28]

Once again, Heidegger claims that when someone feels anxiety, something uncanny (*unheimlich*) is revealed to her. Beings as a whole slip away or recede from her, becoming oppressively present without disappearing. However, this time the uncanny "something" that anxiety reveals through the oppressive receding of beings as a whole is neither *Da-sein*'s essential finitude, nor the contingency of beings as a whole, nor the non-metaphysical event of *beyng*, but rather "the nothing" (*das Nichts*) or absolute nothingness, the possible condition of total non-being in which there is nothing at all.

Finally, in the transcript of a 1962 seminar at Todtnauberg where Heidegger clarifies some themes from his lecture "Time and Being" given earlier that same year, some excerpts from poems by Georg Trakl and Arthur Rimbaud are quoted:

It is a light which the wind has extinguished.

It is a jug which a drunkard leaves in the afternoon.

It is a vineyard, burned and black with holes full of spiders.

It is a room which they have whitewashed.[29]

It is a stubble field on which a black rain falls.

It is a brown tree which stands alone.

It is a hissing wind which circles around empty huts.

It is a light which is extinguished in my mouth.[30]

In the woods there's a bird whose singing stops you and makes you blush.

There's a clock which doesn't strike.

There's a clay pit with a nest of white animals.

There's a cathedral coming down and a lake going up.

There's a little carriage abandoned on the woods or rolling down the path, with ribbons all over it.

There's a troupe of child actors, in costumes, whom you can see on the road through the edge of the wood.

28. Heidegger, "What is Metaphysics?," 101.

29. Guzzoni, "Summary of a Seminar," 39–40.

30. Guzzoni, "Summary of a Seminar," 40.

And there's someone who chases you off when you're hungry and thirst.[31]

Heidegger then comments on the use of "It is" and "They is/are" (*Il y a* in French, *Es gibt* in German) found in these poetic lines:

> First we can say that "It is" confirms the existence of something just as little as the "It gives" [*Es gibt*] does. In contradistinction to the customary one, the "It gives," the "It is" does not name the availability of something which is, but rather precisely something unavailable, what concerns us as something uncanny, the demonic.

As with the other examples of anxiety we have already mentioned, each of the preceding poetic lines evokes in the reader an eerie sense of vague unease in the face if something uncanny, or even "demonic." Yet here the uncanny something in question is either a specific being that does exist, has existed, or might exist: a jug, a whitewashed room, a stubble field, a lone brown tree, a troupe of costumed child actors, and so forth. Thus the uncanny intentional correlate disclosed by each line is typically a particular being distinct from individual *Da-sein*, the totality of beings, non-metaphysical *beyng*, or total nonbeing.

What should we make of the curious elasticity of *Angst*, the fact that at various points throughout his philosophical career Heidegger attributes distinct uncanny intentional correlates to the methodologically central experience of anxiety? One possibility is that anxiety isn't really about anything at all because Heidegger is simply confused. Such a drastic conclusion is premature. Part of the reason why Heidegger's descriptions of anxiety have attracted a wide readership is that these descriptions hone in on what *prima facie* seems to be a genuinely human experience of something deeply unsettling yet quite important. Even if Heidegger himself is sometimes or perhaps always confused about what anxiety is about, the experience's undeniable power nevertheless warrants further phenomenological investigation of it.

Another possibility is that rather than a single experience of anxiety with different intentional correlates, what Heidegger describes is a range of related experiences, each possessing its own distinct intentional correlate. The trouble with this suggestion is that whenever Heidegger talks about anxiety, he always describes it in the same terms: a pervasive dizziness, vertigo, oscillation, and trembling in the face of something uncanny. He thus deprives himself of the finer phenomenological distinctions needed

---

31. Heidegger, *On Time and Being*, 39–40.

to discriminate distinct kinds of noetic experiences correlated with the distinct noemata of uncanny *Da-sein*, the uncanny totality of beings, the uncanny event of non-metaphysical *beyng* (*Ereignis*), uncanny nothingness (*das Nichts*), or the uncanny particularity of some non-human being. If we are to carry forward our investigation of Heidegger's existential phenomenology as it as been presented to us, then we must continue to work with the assumption that whenever Heidegger is discussing anxiety he has only one kind of experience in view.

A third possibility is that anxiety isn't really about what Heidegger thinks it is about but instead gestures toward something else entirely. Let us now explore how the theologian might follow up this suspicion in the course of criticizing Heidegger's existential phenomenology from within.

None of the Above

In his *Itinerarium mentis in Deum*, St. Bonaventure presents the following proof for the existence of God as First Principle.[32] He begins by distinguishing seven trans-categorical characteristics possessed by things in the material universe: being an origin (causing something to exist), magnitude (being extended over a large area), multitude (existing in a plurality), beauty (being aesthetically pleasing), fullness (having the potential to become something else), activity (exercising agency), and order (capable of being numbered, measured, or quantified in other ways). Each of these characteristics is trans-categorical because it is possessed by different kinds of things. For instance, both trees and chimpanzees originate their respective offspring; mountains, oceans, and stars all have magnitude; both schools of whales and flocks of geese are multitudes; Greek Corinthian columns, Bach fugues, and skilled human dancers are all beautiful; and so forth.

Bonaventure next observes that there is a triple property of power, wisdom (or intelligibility), and goodness that is exhibited by things in the material universe insofar as they possess one of the seven trans-categorical characteristics. For example, when the blazing sun originates sprouts by making seeds germinate or a pair of orangutans generate offspring, the sun and the orangutans exhibit causal *power* that is also in each case *intelligible*, since it conforms to comprehensible laws of nature, as well as *good*, since making seeds germinate is beneficial for the creatures who eat them and

---

32. See Bonaventure, *Soul's Journey into God*, 63–68. For a critical discussion of Bonaventure's proof, see Dillard, *Way into Scholasticism*, 16–29.

the orangutans' generating offspring is beneficial for the species. Or to take some other examples, a normal human embryo with fullness or potentiality exhibits a biologically intelligible power to grow into a healthy and long-living adult; the embryo is also good to the extent that it gives rise to the good qualities of health and long life in the adult. Finally, an active charitable organization exhibits power by feeding and clothing the needy, wisdom by being well organized, and goodness by delivering services that are beneficial to the people who need them.

Bonaventure completes the proof by arguing that the triple property of power, wisdom (intelligibility), and goodness is not identical with any of the seven aforementioned trans-categorical characteristics. If, for example, the triple property were identical with magnitude, then any particular material thing could exhibit power, wisdom, and goodness only being extended over a large area, entailing the false consequence that a miniscule human embryo could not exhibit power, wisdom, and goodness. Or if the triple property were identical with multitude, then it would wrongly follow that a single entity such as the sun could not exhibit power, wisdom, and goodness. Similar absurdities would follow if the triple property of power, wisdom, and goodness were the same as being an origin, beauty, fullness, activity, or order. Consequently, power, wisdom, and goodness is a real property that is distinct from any of these characteristics. Bonaventure concludes that what makes the triple property distinct from any trans-categorical characteristic of a material thing—either of something in the material universe or of the material universe itself—is that the triple property is also an attribute of a purely non-material thing: i.e., of God as First Principle. Therefore, God exists.

Bonaventure constructs his proof in the traditional metaphysical context of medieval Scholasticism and Christian Platonism. To be sure, throughout *Sein und Zeit* and elsewhere, Heidegger eschews any metaphysics, traditional or otherwise. Nonetheless, an argument with the same basic pattern as Bonaventure's can be constructed within Heidegger's *Angst*-driven existential phenomenology to show that the intentional correlate of anxiety is an uncanny something completely distinct from any of the intentional correlates Heidegger ascribes to anxiety. Rather than seven trans-categorical characteristics of material things, Heidegger's phenomenology encompasses five ontological conditions: being an individual human in the world (my *Da-sein*), being a particular non-human entity in the world (a jug or a tree or a spider), the totality of all beings in the world (*die Seiende*), the non-metaphysical event of *beyng* or "worlding" itself (*das Ereignis*),[33] and total nonbeing (*das Nichts*). When we are struck by or contemplate any one of these conditions, it is possible for us to experience dizzying, vertiginous, oscillating, and trembling anxiety in the face of something uncanny.

Assume that the uncanny were identical with, say, being an individual human in the world. Then something could be uncanny only by being an individual human, entailing the phenomenologically false consequence that we could never experience uncanniness in the face of a particular non-human entity in the world, the totality of beings, the event of *beyng*, or total nonbeing as uncanny. Or if the uncanny were instead identical with total nonbeing, then none of the other ontological conditions could ever give rise to our experience of anxiety in the face of something uncanny. If the uncanny were identical with any one of Heidegger's five ontological conditions, then similar phenomenological falsehoods would follow. Therefore, the uncanny is distinct from any of the five ontological conditions. What makes the uncanny distinct from *Da-sein*, any specific non-human being, *die Seiende*, *Ereignis*, and *das Nichts* is that, unlike them, the uncanny also pertains primarily to something entirely other than each of these conditions. Faith and theology name this uncanny otherness God, the holy, or divinity.

Before concluding the present chapter, a caveat, two related questions, and an observation are in order. The caveat is that the foregoing internal critique of Heidegger's existential phenomenology should not be read as a *proof* beyond a shadow of the doubt that God exists as an uncanny transcendent something. The reason is that the critique concerns the intentional correlate of anxiety. The intentional correlate of a given experience is what the experience *purports* to be about without prejudging whether it actually exists. I might have a visual experience in which I seem to see a wolf at the edge of the forest, even though in reality there is no wolf there but only a bush at twilight. Of course, I can also have a similar visual experience in which there really is a wolf I see there. In each case, the intentional correlate of my visual experience is a wolf that may or may not be real. The same is true of the experience of anxiety directed toward an uncanny something other than any of the five ontological conditions described by Heidegger. Identifying the intentional correlate of anxiety does not by itself determine whether the correlate is real or not. Nor—at least for the theologian, who is

---

33. Heidegger describes the event of being or appropriation (*Ereignis*) as "worlding" in Heidegger, "Thing," 179–80.

also a person of faith—should it. The point is not to prove God's existence but to underscore how Heidegger's officially agnostic or even atheistic existential phenomenology at its methodological heart is confronted with an open religious question that invites rather than precludes further theological reflection.

One question that immediately arises is: why do we experience anxiety over against a holy something different from any of the ontological conditions described by Heidegger? What makes the divine so *uncanny*? A closely related question follows on the heels of this one. Anytime we experience anxiety, the experience involves either some individualized human existence "thrown" into the world, some particular non-human being, the totality of beings, the non-metaphysical event of *beyng*, or total nonbeing as uncanny. If the proper intentional correlate of anxiety is nonetheless an uncanny divine something distinct from any one of these ontological conditions, then exactly what relationship obtains between the uncanny holy other and the *Angst*-prompting ontological conditions?

An observation suggests where we might hope to find cogent answers to our two questions. In the introduction, we saw that a certain proto-theological picture emerges from Heidegger's *Beiträge zur Philosophie*, according to which "the last god" is neither any specific being, non-being, nor the non-metaphysical event of being ("beyng"). This picture stands in contrast with "Phenomenology and Theology," where Heidegger identifies God with a specific being that is the object of faith and the *positum* of the science of theology. The *Beiträge*'s proto-theological picture also gibes with the result of our internal critique, which argues that the intentional correlate of *Angst* is an uncanny holy something other than any specific human or non-human being, the totality of beings, total non-being, and the event of *beyng*. Therefore, in seeking further answers, we do well to turn our attention to one of Heidegger's most difficult yet potentially rewarding works.

Chapter 4

Coming to Terms with Heidegger's *Contributions*

> It must nevertheless be possible to provide a first naming and reference to *Da-sein* and thereby an indication of it. To be sure, that could never be an immediate "description," as if *Da-sein* were simply to be found objectively present somewhere; nor could it be through a "dialectic," which is the same approach on a higher level.[1]

TWO DIAGRAMS

PHILOSOPHICAL DISCUSSIONS OF INTENTIONALITY often feature the following standard diagram:

noesis ———> noema[2]

The diagram is accompanied by an interpretation of its elements. The noesis is a particular act of experiencing like seeing, hearing, or imagining. The bearer of the experience is a subject, a concrete "I" or self who does the experiencing. The noema is the intentional correlate of the subject's act of experiencing, the purported object, thing, or being toward which the act is directed. The arrow stands for the property of the subject's noesis in virtue of which it directed toward the noema. So, for example, if I hear a

1. Heidegger, *Contributions to Philosophy*, 244.
2. See, for example, Idhe, *Experimental Phenomenology*, 26.

sparrow singing, I am the experiencing subject or self, my act of hearing is the noesis, and the singing sparrow is the noema toward which my act of hearing is directed. Indeed, we encountered the noesis-noema terminology in the previous chapter.

In the *Beiträge*, Heidegger presents a very different diagram when he is discussing human intentionality:

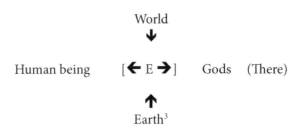

Why does Heidegger prefer his diagram? The standard diagram and its accompanying interpretation seem fairly straightforward. By contrast, Heidegger's diagram looks extremely puzzling. Initially, it is far from clear how the terms "world," "earth," and the arrows between them should be interpreted. Moreover, Heidegger's diagram seems to leave out the experiencing subject, "the ego (thinking self) thinking what is thought."[4] Although the term "human being" occurs on one side of the diagram, it stands opposite the plural term "gods" on the other side, implying that "human being" signifies humanity in general as opposed to a specific human individual or self. And what do the "gods" over "there" have to do with anything?

Heidegger's remark, quoted at the beginning of this chapter, that although a preliminary indication of *Da-sein* is possible, it is not a description of *Da-sein* as objectively present somewhere, comes immediately before Heidegger presents his own diagram. Then, in the following section, he gives a preliminary indication of *Da-sein*:

> *Da-sein* is the axis in the turning of the event, the self-opening center of the counterplay between calling and belonging. *Da-sein* is the "domain of what is proper [*Eigen-tum*, "property], understood in analogy with the "domain of a prince" [*Fürsten-tum*, "principality"], the sovereign center of the appropriating eventuation as the assignment, of the ones who belong, to the event and at

3. See Heidegger, *Contributions to Philosophy*, 246. Heidegger's diagram has been slightly altered in order to streamline it a bit.

4. Idhe, *Experimental Phenomenology*, 27.

the same time to themselves: becoming a self. Thus, *Da-sein* is the
between: between humans (as grounding of history) and the gods
(in their history).[5]

Admittedly, these remarks are somewhat cryptic. Even so, they suggest how
we should approach both the standard diagram and the diagram preferred
by Heidegger.

There is nothing intrinsically wrong with the standard diagram as
shorthand for the truism that human beings experience singing sparrows,
trees, streams, and many other beings in the world around them. However, the accompanying interpretation skates over important philosophical
questions. Is the experiencing self already given, or is the self something
yet to be attained? Notice that Heidegger associates *Da-sein* with selfhood.
He insists that no description of *Da-sein* as objectively present is possible;
instead, *Da-sein* involves *becoming* a self. If so, then human beings cannot
take selfhood for granted but can only try or at least hope to acquire it.
Da-sein is a challenge, not a given. Heidegger's analogy between *Da-sein's*
proper domain and the domain of a prince is instructive. Instead of princedom as a generic condition, let us imagine somebody who succeeds in being a proper prince. Being a proper prince is not a pre-given, objectively
present foregone conclusion but a role, identity, or self that emerges only in
an ongoing attempt to rule effectively. Furthermore, particular beings—the
realm, the material resources to sustain and defend it, vassals, serfs, and the
wolf as its royal insignia—are only experienced as such in the context of
this ongoing attempt. Thus Heidegger also questions the interpretation of
noemata as pre-given objects of experience.[6]

To the extent that Heidegger associates *Da-sein* with selfhood, his
preliminary indication of *Da-sein* as "between" humans and gods means
that the experiencing self is not absent from his diagram. It is located right
in the middle of the diagram along the axis between "world" and "earth":
"*Da-sein is the occurrence of the sundering of the axis for the turning of the
event*."[7] By "the event," Heidegger has in mind a radically non-metaphysical
orientation to being that eventually might come to supplant the various

5. Heidegger, *Contributions to Philosophy*, 246–47.

6. Heidegger is not propounding some version of metaphysical idealism, according
to which external objects are purely mental constructs. This landmass, these minerals,
plants, and animals, and those people are not ideas in the prince's mind. Yet these entities
do not stand out, respectively, as a realm, its resources, and its subjects apart from the
prince's ongoing attempt to rule effectively.

7. Heidegger, *Contributions to Philosophy*, 246.

metaphysical conceptions of being that have hitherto dominated the history of the West. Somehow, *Da-sein* or genuine selfhood emerges from generic human being, setting up a sundering struggle between world and earth in which divinity might be encountered as vividly "there."

Already we can begin to see why Heidegger's *Beiträge* philosophy could prove to be a useful tool in our project of developing a theology of *Streit*. The philosophy and the envisioned theology share a decidedly non-metaphysical impulse, an emphasis on struggle, and a willingness to construe divinity in highly unconventional terms. But first, several formidable hurdles must be overcome. One is the often turgid and opaque style of Heidegger's text. Additionally, as will become evident in the course of the present chapter, once Heidegger's principal philosophical "contribution" is expressed in clear language, it teeters on the edge of total vacuity. Two possible ways to avoid this vacuity are available to Heidegger: the notion of "time-space," and the need to make a definite decision that results either in the epiphany or remaining hidden of the last god. Unfortunately, time-space is ultimately just another instance of the kind of metaphysics that Heidegger rejects. Only the specific commitment of having to decide about the last god injects definite content into Heidegger's post-metaphysical vision without reintroducing metaphysics, a result that indicates the indispensability of religious concerns to the *Beiträge*. We will then be in a better position both to appropriate the relevant philosophical aspects of that work as well as to appreciate the distinctively theological challenge it confronts.

Commitment, Interdependency, and Tautology

Early in the *Beiträge*, Heidegger describes what he considers to be "the guiding question" of Western philosophy from its inception to Nietzsche:

> It most general form was impressed on it by Aristotle: what is τί τὸ ὄν; (What are beings?). That is to say, for Aristotle: what is οὐσία as the beingness of beings? Here being means *beingness*. Expressed at once therein is this: despite the denial that being has the character of a genus, nevertheless being (as beingness) is always and only meant as the κοινόν, the common and thus what is common to every being.[8]

---

8. Heidegger, *Contributions to Philosophy*, 60.

Heidegger regards the guiding question as quintessentially metaphysical. The philosopher asks what is the maximally general characteristic common to all and only beings. This characteristic is then identified with being or "beingness." Depending on the philosopher, being is identified with a different maximally general characteristic. Perhaps being is identified with super-sensibility (Plato), actuality (Aristotle), with what is capable of being an object of representational judgment (Kant), with a phase in the development of Absolute Spirit (Hegel), or with whatever the Übermensch wills to recur eternally (Nietzsche). In each case, the guiding question starts with beings and then moves on the being as what is common to them all.

By contrast, what Heidegger calls "the basic question" does not start with beings but instead tries to "leap" directly into the truth of *beyng* construed not as the maximal characteristic common to beings but as the non-metaphysical event (*Ereignis*):

> With the question of *beyng*, on the other hand, the starting point is not beings, i.e., this or that given being, nor is it beings as such and as a whole; instead, what us carried out is a leap into the *truth* (clearing and concealing) of *beyng* itself.[9]

Heidegger thinks that the event has been occurring all along, even when different answers to the guiding question have been given in the history of Western philosophy. But since they all treat being as fixed characteristic ("beingness") rather than as a dynamic happening, these metaphysical answers provide only a distorted understanding of the event. The *Beiträge's* task is to set the stage for an undistorted understanding of it by pursuing the basic question. Since Heidegger regards the event "as the ground in which all beings first come to their truth (sheltering, instituting, objectivity),"[10] once an undistorted understanding of the event is attained, beings will emerge not as objects of judgment or willing but undistorted as non-objectified nature, artworks, tools, and deeds "sheltering" the event.[11]

Already with his discussion of "circumspection" in *Sein und Zeit*, Heidegger lays the groundwork for a non-metaphysical understanding of the event further developed in the *Beiträge*. He uses the example of craftsmen

---

9. Heidegger, *Contributions to Philosophy*, 60.

10. Heidegger, *Contributions to Philosophy*, 61.

11. See where Heidegger speaks of nature as resting "in the original occurrence of *beyng* itself" (Heidegger, *Contributions to Philosophy*, 218) and where the event "sets truth into work, into tool, and it [*Da-sein*] experiences truth as a thing, consummates truth in deed and sacrifice" (Heidegger, *Contributions to Philosophy*, 308).

laboring in a workshop.[12] Their particular project of making a pair of shoes for a customer or building a clock for the town hall allows various beings such as tools (hammer, tongs, plane, needle) and materials (steel, iron, metal, wood) to be grasped reflexively as relevant to the task being undertaken.[13] From the perspective of the *Beiträge*, these beings come to their undistorted truth through the unfolding of a specific event: namely, the craftsmen undertaking to make the shoes or the clock. As *Da-sein*, the craftsmen do not start with the relevant beings and then extrapolate back to the undertaking as the maximally general characteristic the beings share. Instead, it is *Da-sein*'s "leap" into a specific undertaking that allows tools and materials to emerge as a rich and irreducible diversity of relevant beings in the first place.[14]

Yet if there were nothing more to non-metaphysical being than the sort of circumspection described in *Sein und Zeit*, a certain danger would arise. So far, circumspection seems to be a thoroughly anthropocentric affair, since everything is structured around *Da-sein*'s decisions to pursue specific undertakings or projects. But then all beings share the maximally general characteristic of being at *Da-sein*'s disposal for the fulfillment of its own objectives. To be is to be a potential resource for human consumption. In later work, Heidegger refers to this totalizing metaphysical conception in which human beings employ increasingly sophisticated technology in order to control and exploit tools, materials, plants, animals, and even other humans ("human resources") for human purposes as "enframing" (*Ge-stell*).[15] We can begin to think beyond it, he suggests, by observing how the emergence of enframing itself is *not* something entirely under human control.

---

12. See Heidegger, *Being and Time*, 62–67.

13. Heidegger refers to a particular project as the primary "what-for" or "for-the-sake-of-which." See Heidegger, *Being and Time*, 78.

14. With respect to a specific undertaking like a workshop project, Heidegger urges that an experience of beings as "objectively present" only occurs in the atypical case when something either breaks down or is missing. Hence *objective presence* cannot function as a maximally general characteristic applying to all and only beings in the workshop in the typical case when everything is running smoothly. See Heidegger, *Being and Time*, 67–71.

15. For example: "Enframing means the gathering together of that setting-upon which sets upon man, i.e., challenges him forth, to reveal the real, in the mode of ordering, as standing-reserve" (Heidegger, "Question Concerning Technology," 20).

[Enframing] is the way in which the real reveals itself as standing-reserve. Again we ask: Does this revealing happen somewhere beyond all human doing? No. But neither does it happen exclusively *in* man or decisively *through* man.[16]

Coming to treat all beings are resources controlled and exploited by *Da-sein* is not itself a resource controlled and exploited by *Da-sein*. To be sure, it cannot take place totally apart from *Da-sein*. Nonetheless, the emergence of enframing is not something that *Da-sein* orchestrates or a piece of "standing-reserve" at *Da-sein*'s disposal, revealing a lacuna in the modern metaphysics of technological consumerism.

In the *Beiträge*, Heidegger reinforces the step back from the hyper-humanism of enframing with the observation that *Da-sein* itself arises out of the non-controllable event of appropriation and hence is also not something completely under its own control:

> The projection at issue is always the one of the truth of beyng. The very projector, *Da-sein*, is thrown—i.e., appropriated—by *beyng*. Inasmuch as the projector projects and opens up the openness, this opening reveals that the projector himself is thrown and accomplishes nothing but the catching hold of the oscillation in *beyng*, i.e., the entrance into the oscillation and thereby into the event, and so first becomes the projector, namely, the preserver of the thrown projection.[17]

Here and throughout the *Beiträge*, "*Da-sein*" does not means what it does in *Sein und Zeit*, where the term is used to designate individualized human being that can either lose itself in inauthenticity or own up to its essential finitude in resolute authenticity. Instead, "*Da-sein*" now designates being a genuine seeker, preserver, and steward of the non-metaphysical event.[18]

Unfortunately, whether one begins with *Da-sein* or with the event, Heidegger's characterization of the intimate relation between them threatens to collapse into empty tautology. Suppose we begin with *Da-sein*. Thrown *Da-sein* is the projecting and opening up of the event, which in turn is what reveals *Da-sein* as thrown projector. So thrown *Da-sein* is the projecting and opening up of what reveals *Da-sein* as thrown projector.[19]

16. Heidegger, "Question Concerning Technology," 23–24.

17. Heidegger, *Contributions to Philosophy*, 240.

18. See also Heidegger, *Contributions to Philosophy*, 16.

19. According to Kenneth Maly, "Since *what* is projected by *Da-sein*, the tender [i.e., preserver], is the essential swaying of be-ing as enowning [i.e., the event], what *Da-sein*

Alternatively, suppose we begin with the appropriating event as the opening that reveals *Da-sein*. Since *Da-sein* is nothing but the projecting and opening up of appropriating event, the appropriating event is the opening that reveals what projects and opens up the appropriating event.[20] These descriptions of thrown *Da-sein* and the appropriating event are as uninformative as they are uncontroversial. For they do not tell us exactly *who Da-sein* is supposed to be or precisely *what* is supposed to happen in the event.

Some of Heidegger's remarks about language do offer a slightly more informative characterization of the relation between *Da-sein* and the non-metaphysical event of appropriation. Heidegger regards language as a multifaceted phenomenon defined by two poles. On the one hand, "language shows itself first as our way of speaking," and "Speaking must have speakers, but not merely in the same way as an effect must have a cause."[21] The manifold expressions of a living language with the complexity of German, French, or English cannot possess the linguistic meanings they do unless highly intelligent human beings use particular sounds and inscriptions in specific ways. On the other hand, "the ability to speak is what marks man as man."[22] There cannot be humans possessing a high level of intelligence apart from a fairly sophisticated language they have mastered. Language neither causes human beings nor do human beings cause language comparable to how fire causes smoke. Rather, human beings and language in the fullest sense are interdependent. Moreover, in learning their native language, humans not only acquire linguistic knowledge but also gain a basic understanding of the world and their place in it; as Heidegger provocatively

---

preserves or tends is be-ing's enowning of *Da-sein*" (Maly, "Turnings in Essential Swaying and the Leap," 161). This extremely tight rhetorical circle comes close to saying nothing more than that what *Da-sein* preserves or tends is the event of *Da-sein*'s preserving and tending.

20. Richard Polt identifies *Da-sein*'s non-metaphysical "enthinking" of the enowning event with the kind poetic naming exemplified by Hölderlin, where this "poetic naming is the happening of enowning in language" (Polt, "Event of Enthinking the Event," 97). When enowning happens essentially, then, it is grasped in a poetic manner undistorted by metaphysics. What is the undistorted manner of grasping enowning? It is the happening of enowning in language—leaving us with the triviality that enowning happens essentially when enowning is grasped through the happening of enowning in language. In fairness to Polt, he fully recognizes that "we may find ourselves at a loss for words when we try to speak the language of pure be-ing" (Polt, "Event of Enthinking the Event," 97). Heidegger's tautologies are perhaps symptomatic of this loss for words.

21. Heidegger, "Way to Language," 120.

22. Heidegger, "Way to Language," 112.

states, "Language speaks by saying, that is, by showing."[23] Thus the interdependency that Heidegger has in view obtains between humans as thinking beings and language as revelatory of reality.

It is important to keep this interdependency firmly in mind in order to ward off certain ways of misconceiving the relation between human beings and language—including one that Heidegger himself sometimes flirts with, as will become clear in a later chapter. But in the present context, where we are primarily concerned with improving upon Heidegger's sketchy characterizations of *Da-sein* and the non-metaphysical event of being or appropriation, the aforementioned interdependency is insufficient. Merely reflecting on how thinking human beings both enable and are enabled by complex language disclosing a general understanding of the world does not tell us who we are, what language we speak, what its expressions mean, or how the world actually is. Heidegger's assurance that language speaks by saying and showing says and shows nothing definite about *Da-sein's* seeking and preserving stewardship, what transpires in the unfolding of the event, and how *Da-sein* and the event are non-trivially interrelated. Little if any progress has been made beyond Heidegger's earlier, tautological characterizations.

Part of the problem is that Heidegger attempts to describe the interrelation between *Da-sein* and the non-metaphysical event of appropriation at a level that is far too general and abstract. It may be more helpful instead to focus on the interdependency between a given role or identity and various beings standing out within the context of a particular project or commitment. Recall the example of the prince. Certainly there can be no such beings as the princely realm, the royal army and navy suitable for its defense, vassals, serfs, or royal insignias apart from someone trying to be a successful prince. Yet the possibility of being a successful prince is equally dependent on the availability of these beings. To take another example, a tract of land only stands out as an environmental preserve containing protected woodlands, designated wetlands, and endangered species in relation to a group of people who undertake the commitment of being wardens. But the ongoing commitment to be a warden can only unfold against the backdrop of an environmental preserve. The particular interdependency

23. Heidegger, "Way to Language," 124. In a similar vein, Wittgenstein comments on how a child learning its native language "learns to believe a host of things, i.e., it learns to act according to these beliefs. Bit by bit there forms a system of what is believed, and in that system some things stand unshakably fast and some are more or less liable to shift" (Wittgenstein, *On Certainty*, 21).

between princedom and realm or between wardenship and environmental preserve means that we do not first understand what one of these things and then use it to define the other; rather, we only understand what these things are together. In this regard, Wittgenstein's comment that "Light dawns gradually over the whole"[24] is apt. By forsaking windy generalization and concentrating instead on particular human projects or commitments, perhaps we will be able to arrive at a more concrete characterization of *Da-sein* in relation to the non-metaphysical event. Heidegger himself suggests two very different ways of doing so that will be considered in the next two sections.

Time-Space and Metaphysics

Section 242 of the *Beiträge* contains the heart of Heidegger's difficult reflections on so-called "abyssal ground" (*Abgrund*):

> The abyssal ground is the hesitant self-withholding of the ground. In this withholding, the originary emptiness opens up and originary *clearing* occurs, but this clearing is such that, at the same time, hesitation is manifest in it.[25]

The abyssal ground is an invariant structure of self-withholding that is operative in any human project. This self-withholding structure has both a temporal and a spatial aspect. Each aspect can be illustrated in connection with the two particular projects we have already mentioned.

Heidegger describes the temporal manifestation of the abyssal ground as follows:

> The self-withholding creates not only the *emptiness* of privation and austerity but also, along with these, an emptiness as one that is in itself transporting, i.e., transporting into the "to come" and thereby simultaneously bursting open what has been. The latter, by making an impact together with what is to come, constitutes the present as a move into the abandonment that remembers and expects.[26]

Someone cannot currently pursue the project of trying to be a successful prince or an effective warden unless the historical past has already made

---

24. Wittgenstein, *On Certainty*, 21.

25. Heidegger, *Contributions to Philosophy*, 300.

26. Heidegger, *Contributions to Philosophy*, 303.

princedom and wardenship available as possible human roles. The project must also be "transported" or oriented toward the future in which successful princedom or effective wardenship will either have been achieved or missed. Yet Heidegger takes these past and future dimensions to be related to the present in an even deeper manner. The past in which princedom (or wardenship) are mere human possibilities that no one is pursuing must withhold itself from the present; otherwise, the present would be exactly like this past, and hence no one would be currently pursuing either project. The future in which successful princedom (effective wardenship) has either been achieved or missed must also withhold itself from the present; otherwise, the present would be exactly like this future, so that the person in question would no longer be pursuing the relevant project but instead would have already finished trying to execute it. Through the joint operation of their respective withholdings, then, past and future open up a specific present.

Heidegger describes the spatial manifestation of the abyssal ground as a kind of captivation:

> The self-withholding dispenses the transporting which is characteristic of the temporalizing, but, as *hesitant*, it is also the most originary *captivation* of things. This captivation is the *embrace* in which the moment and thus the temporalization are held fast.[27]

Trying to be a successful prince or an effective warden may involve scaling a mountain (either to scout out an army of foreign invaders bivouacking in the valley below or to investigate whether the trees on the slope have been damaged by acid rain). In either case, the mountain to be scaled provides a site for currently pursuing the relevant project. In order to function as such a site, the mountain must withhold its summit and slopes; otherwise, like the ground immediately under our feet, the mountain in its entirely would be already given, thereby foreclosing any need to scale it.[28]

Heidegger proceeds to identify the abyssal ground's self-withholding of temporal and spatial dimensions that allows human beings to be in the process of pursuing any particular project with the event of appropriation,

---

27. Heidegger, *Contributions to Philosophy*, 303.

28. Heidegger sometimes describes the abyssal ground's spatial self-withholding as the earth's recalcitrance to becoming fully disclosed: "The earth appears openly cleared as itself only when it is perceived and preserved as that which by nature is undisclosable, that which from every disclosure and constantly keeps itself closed up" (Heidegger, "Origin of the Work of Art," 47).

and he identifies *Da-sein* with human beings who clearly grasp how self-withholding is at work in their current activities:

> Since truth is the clearing concealment of beyng, however, it is as abyssal ground chiefly a ground that grounds only as bearing and allowing the protruding of the event. For the hesitant withholding is the intimation that *beckons Da-sein*, and this latter is precisely the constancy of clearing concealment. This occurrence is the oscillation of the turning between call and belonging; it is ap-*propriation*, beyng itself.[29]

The event as the self-withholding of temporal and spatial dimensions is always occurring, whether human beings recognize its exact nature or not. If and when they *do* come to recognize temporal and spatial self-withholding for what it really is, they will see that it has nothing to do with Platonic super-sensibility, Aristotelian actuality, Kantian representational judgment, Hegelian Absolute Spirit, Nietzschean Eternal Recurrence, or any of the other metaphysical conceptions have dominated different eras of Western philosophy. Then the event will occur *essentially* because its non-metaphysical character of self-withholding will be truly understood, and human beings will become *Da-sein* because they have attained a true insight into the nature of the event.

The trouble is that—despite Heidegger's repeated assurances to the contrary—*abyssal self-withholding* is just another metaphysical conception of being. Heidegger wants "to make visible in an interpretation the spatiality and temporality of thing, tool, work, machination, and of every being, as modes of sheltering the truth" where "the projection of this interpretation is tacitly determined by the knowledge of time-space as the abyss."[30] Every being is temporal and spatial in the mode of abyssal self-withholding as "the *originary unity* of space and time."[31] Therefore, at the most general level every being is characterized by abyssal self-withholding imparted through its temporal and spatial aspects. The latter conclusion is confirmed by the observation that no rock, plant, animal, human, or any other being is ever given all at once but instead withholds temporal and spatial aspects of itself. With a speculative inexorability reminiscent of Spinoza, Heidegger begins with beings, moves to their temporality and spatiality, and finally isolates the maximally general characteristic of abyssal withholding latent

29. Heidegger, *Contributions to Philosophy*, 300.
30. Heidegger, *Contributions to Philosophy*, 306.
31. Heidegger, *Contributions to Philosophy*, 299.

within time-space as common to all beings. For this reason, the first way that Heidegger suggests of characterizing the event (i.e., as abyssal self-withholding) and *Da-sein* (i.e., as human beings who truly grasp abyssal self-withholding) lapses back into the very kind of metaphysical thinking he seeks to avoid.[32]

A Non-Metaphysical Commitment and a Religious Decision

The second way of bringing the interdependency between the event of appropriation and *Da-sein* down to earth is suggested by something else Heidegger says in section 242 of the *Beiträge*:

> That which opens itself for concealment is originally the remoteness of the undecidability clinging to the question of whether the god is moving away or toward us. That means: in this remoteness and its undecidability, there is manifest the concealment of that which, on account of this opening, is called god.[33]

To avoid the empty verbiage of Heidegger's highly abstruse generalizations concerning *Da-sein*, the event, and their interrelation, we saw how it helped to concentrate on the interdependency between roles and beings in a particular undertaking like princedom or wardenship. Obviously *Da-sein* is not reducible to being a proper prince or an effective warden, and the event of appropriation is not reducible to the flourishing of a royal realm or an environmental preserve. Yet in the above passage, Heidegger implies that there is a specific project or commitment in which the terms "*Da-sein*" and "the event" acquire meanings as definite as the terms "prince" or "warden" and "realm" or "preserve": namely, the need for us to decide whether the god is moving away or toward us.

What part does the event play in the project of deciding about the last god? As Heidegger repeatedly emphasizes, clearing as freedom from

32. In his last writings, Heidegger depicts the event of appropriation and our relation to it quite differently. Rather that something latent within time and space, appropriation is now understood is now understood as something that *sends* both the time and space in which humans dwell. The self-withholding or "extending" of temporal and spatial dimensions stands in either a univocal or an analogical relation to the self-withholding of appropriation that sends them. See especially Heidegger, "Time and Being." For a critique of Heidegger's late notion of appropriation see Dillard, *Heidegger and Philosophical Atheology*, 57–70.

33. Heidegger, *Contributions to Philosophy*, 302.

distortion is essential to the event in its non-metaphysical occurrence. In order to decide about the last god, human beings must first become free from any metaphysical or other philosophical distortions in their thinking about divinity. Rather than happening all at once, this deconstructive (or as Wittgenstein might say, therapeutic) process unfolds gradually over time. Perhaps, as will be argued in the next chapter, it includes overcoming the eschatological and harmatiological problems found in St. Paul and Luther. The proponent of *Streit* theology takes the upshot to be a growing sense of relief and expectancy in the realization that the fewer misconceptions one has about divinity, the better prepared one is to make a lucid and crucial decision about it. Thus in line with the proto-theological picture informing the basic narrative of the *Beiträge*, the non-metaphysical event of *beyng* is not the same as the last god but instead an occurrence that sets the stage for a human decision that will result in the last god's either absconding or appearing.

A king's son who over time successfully rules a royal realm becomes a true prince. A trustee who over time effectively safeguards an environmental preserve becomes a true warden. True princedom and true wardenship are distinctive forms of human selfhood over and above generic human being. No prince or warden ever attains absolute perfection, since in the course of these respective pursuits it is always possible for additional challenges to arise or for matters to have been handled even better. Similarly, someone who perseveres in clearing away metaphysical or other philosophical distortions becomes what Heidegger in the *Beiträge* calls *Da-sein*:

> *Da-sein* is the steadfast enduring of the clearing, i.e., of the freed, unprotected, the belonging domain of the "there" wherein *beyng* conceals itself. The steadfast enduring of the clearing of self-concealing is taken up in the seeking, preserving, and stewardship carried out by *that* human being who has self-knowledge as one appropriated to being and belonging of the event qua the essential occurrence of *beyng*.[34]

Like true princedom and true wardenship, *Da-sein* is a kind of human selfhood beyond generic humanity that emerges through a sustained seeking, preserving, and stewarding of clarity in our thinking about ourselves, our place in the world, and divinity. No matter how long or how well we execute this custodial task and hence succeed in becoming *Da-sein*, "there" always

---

34. Heidegger, *Contributions to Philosophy*, 235.

remains the possibility that we could have done a better job or that "there" are other confusions concerning these topics that we have overlooked.

The quotation marks just used are intended to indicate what Heidegger in the previous passage describes as that "wherein *beyng* conceals itself." Elsewhere in the pivotal section 242 of the *Beiträge*, Heidegger speaks of "the uniqueness of *beyng* and its inexhaustibility."[35] We can now give a non-trivial characterization of *Da-sein*, *beyng*, and the interdependency between them. *Da-sein* is the selfhood of seeking and preserving stewardship that emerges in the specific, ongoing task of clearing away conceptual confusions. Once *Da-sein* has emerged in a few thoughtful people or even an entire people, *beyng* is never exhausted since the potential for removing confusions always outstrips whatever confusions we have actually removed in two ways: (1) there is always the possibility of new confusions that could be removed, and (2) there is always the possibility that many if not all of the confusions that have been removed could have been removed better (sooner, more articulately, or less cumbersomely). *Beyng* is the unique two-fold phenomenon consisting of the ever-expanding clearing—i.e., more and more removed confusions—and the self-concealing—i.e., the potential for removing confusions encompassing (1) and (2). *Da-sein* depends on *beyng*, since there is no confusion-removing selfhood without removed confusions. Courtesy of its ever-expanding clearing aspect, *beyng* also depends on *Da-sein*, since there is no removing of more and more confusions without confusion-removing selves who remove them. Nonetheless, *beyng* in its self-concealing inexhaustibility outstrips *Da-sein* in both its individual and communal manifestations.

Once an apprentice has felled enough trees to form a clearing in the forest, he/she emerges as a successful woodsman who may now decide whether or not to build a house there. According to viewpoint of the *Beiträge*, when enough distortions have been cleared away for *Da-sein* to emerge from generic human being, *Da-sein* must then make a distinct decision that results in the last god's either absconding or appearing. Heidegger goes so far to refer to the need for this decision as the strife between the last god and the human being:

> The former belonging [of *Da-sein*] to *beyng* and the latter needing [by the god] of *beyng* first reveal *beyng* in its self-concealment as that turning center in which the belonging surpasses the needing and the needing protrudes beyond the belonging: *beyng* as

35. Heidegger, *Contributions to Philosophy*, 302.

appropriating event, which happens out of this turning excess of itself and thus becomes the origin of the strife between the god and the human being, between the passing by of the god and the history of mankind.[36]

In order to "pass by" or vividly appear to humans, the last god needs the clearing work of *beyng* to remove human misconceptions about divinity. But the clearing work is not sufficient for the last god to appear. *Da-sein* must still make the necessary decision about the last god through strife with it. In terms of Heidegger's diagram of intentionality, the *Streit* theologian locates this striving decision in the crosshairs between world and earth where *Da-sein* struggles to gain an illuminating experience of divinity in the face of divine obscurity.[37]

Many questions remain. Exactly how is *Da-sein* supposed to make the decision about divinity that is required of it? Why does Heidegger sometimes speak of the gods in the plural, while at other times he only mentions one last god? Before answering these questions, let us apply the clearing work of *beyng* to two specific problems that have arisen in the course of our theological project.

---

36. Heidegger, *Contributions to Philosophy*, 327.

37. The *Gelassenheit* theologian interprets Heidegger's diagram differently. She takes the crosshairs between world and earth to mark the ongoing struggle to divest our thinking about divinity of metaphysical and other conceptual confusions in preparation for *Da-sein*'s experiencing the holy as an energized tranquility that can guide *Da-sein* to make decisions under the holy's influence.

Chapter 5

Theological Progress and a
Theological Predicament

*Allerdings ist diese Angst vielleicht nicht nur Angst, sondern auch
Sehnsucht nach etwas, was mehr ist als alles Angsterregende.*[1]

DEFLATING DOUBTS

IT IS ONE THING to be immersed in a project but something else to step back
from it in order to provide the project with a rationale. Some rationales
are problematic because instead of giving the project a proper foundation,
they raise crippling doubts that threaten to undermine it. The task of the
ever-expanding clearing work through which the seeking and preserving
stewardship of *Da-sein* emerges is to safeguard the project or commitment
of deciding about the last god by deflating such doubts. Let us begin by
considering how clearing work might be useful in connection with some
other possible projects.

Suppose that someone committed to being a proper prince gives
the following rationale for his project. He believes that by divine right, a
king and his designated heirs may acquire as much land as they want and
can efficiently administer. Since his father is a king and he is his father's
designated heir, this divine right to aggressive expansion transfers to the

1. "However, perhaps this anxiety is not only anxiety but also yearning for something more than everything arousing anxiety" (Franz Kafka quoted in Killy, "Nachwort,"
167).

prince. So he sets off to conquer additional territory, perhaps an island in the Pacific Ocean. However, there is another king with a princess who harbors the same beliefs about her father and herself and who is also intent on conquering the same island. Apprised by his foreign minister of her convictions and plans, the hapless prince is plunged into confusion. If he tries to conquer the island himself, is he fulfilling or violating God's will? The prince finds himself paralyzed by doubt until a wise counselor debunks the whole notion of divine right. Freed from that illusion, the prince is able to decide whether or not to fight the princess for the island based on feasibility, expense, competing priorities, and other practical factors.

Next, imagine that while pursuing their commitment to environmental preservation of a tract of land, a group of wardens is confronted with the following challenge. Poachers have been excessively hunting the forests and fishing the streams on the tract, to the point that many species of wildlife there are becoming endangered. The wardens meet to decide how they should respond. It seems obvious that the proper course of action is to undertake steps to stop the poachers, perhaps by appointing rangers to patrol the tract. A warden then gives a deep-ecological rationale: like human beings, nature itself has inherent rights that moral agents have a duty to respect and protect. One of nature's inherent rights is for its wildlife not to be wantonly plundered. The poachers are violating this right and hence should be stopped by appointing rangers to patrol the natural tract of land. Another warden who has been nervously shifting in her chair replies that the poachers are also animals, albeit highly intelligent ones. As such, they do not stand outside of nature but are an integral part of it. How are they violating one of nature's inherent rights by hunting and fishing, anymore than a pride of lions violates one of nature's inherent rights by hunting an entire pack of gazelles? The meeting is immediately thrown into consternation. It would certainly help if somebody pointed out philosophical difficulties with the very idea of deep ecology, or at least with attempting to apply it to the present case.

Sometimes Heidegger's own descriptions of the interdependency between *Da-sein* and *beyng* spawn doubt instead of allaying it:

> Appropriation [*Eignung*] is at once assignment [*Zu-eignung*] and consignment [*Übereignung*]. Inasmuch as *Da-sein* is assigned to *itself* as belonging to the event, *Da-sein* does come to its *self*, but never as if the self were already an objectively present item that simply had not been previously reached. Rather, *Da-sein* comes to

itself first precisely when the assignment to the belonging becomes at once a consignment into the event.[2]

Here the sticking point is Heidegger's assignment-consignment rhetoric. Given my fledgling talent for removing conceptual distortions, I might believe I have been assigned the task of becoming *Da*-sein by participating in the clearing work of *beyng*.[3] Whether or not I succeed depends on the outcome of my deflationary endeavors; in this sense, I am consigned to *beyng*. All at once, I am gripped with uncertainty. What if I never remove confusions or only remove a few? What if I do remove a considerable number of distortions but could have removed even more or could have removed the ones I did more adroitly? Then maybe I wasn't really assigned to participate in the clearing work or *beyng* in the first place! Once Heidegger's talk of "the intrinsically conjoined assignment and consignment"[4] is set aside, this particular puzzle seems not to arise.

Although these preliminary examples may be useful in fixing ideas, they run the risk of oversimplification. It is not enough merely to dismiss a problematic rationale for a given project on the purely pragmatic ground that the rationale in question interferes with our pursuit of the project. The prince who wishes to conquer the island might be deeply committed to the notion of divine right, in which case the counselor's debunking of that notion will be convincing only if it is skillfully executed. If the warden who appeals to deep ecology as a rationale for appointing rangers to protect the tract from poachers finds that environmental philosophy intellectually compelling, then a successful deflation of it in connection with the ranger issue must be even more compelling intellectually. Finally, even if Heidegger's consignment-assignment description of interdependent *Da*-sein and *beyng* is by no means obligatory, there is still the need to supply some other concrete description of the interdependency that is not vulnerable to the same doubt. The last chapter began to do so by linking the interdependency between *Da*-sein and *beyng* to the specific religious commitment of making a decision that results in the last god's absconding or appearing. Whether this alternative approach avoids the kind of doubt affecting Heidegger's talk of assignment and consignment remains to be determined. The theological conundrums we encountered in Paul and Luther can serve

2. Heidegger, *Contributions to Philosophy*, 253.

3. Analogously, someone might believe that her fledgling talent "assigns" or demands from her the task of becoming a master artist by creating great art.

4. Heidegger, *Contributions to Philosophy*, 253.

as a testing ground for the emergence of *Da-sein* through the clearing work of the *Beiträge* in preparation for making a decision about the last god.

The Sacred Clock and What Happens in Its Own Time

In chapter 2, we saw how the radically new vision of time that Heidegger detects in St. Paul's eschatology threatens to drown the passionate excitement of primitive Christian experience in doubt. If the Christian present between Christ's resurrection and Christ's promised return is simultaneously a recapitulation of Christ's earthly life and a running toward something that continues not to happen, then the same Christian present is increasingly dominated by the frustration and disappointment of an unfulfilled expectation. Eventually the burden may become too heavy to bear, leading to skepticism, indifference, and apostasy. Thus the availability of philosophical resources suitable for unraveling this paradox without generating metaphysical quandaries would be most welcome to the eschatological theologian. Can such resources be found in Heidegger's *Beiträge*?

Early on in the work, Heidegger makes a striking remark:

> All beginnings are in themselves what is unsurpassably complete. They escape historiology not because they are supra-temporal, eternal, but rather because they are greater than eternity: *the strokes of time* which grant to being the openness of its self-concealment. The proper grounding of this time-space is *Da-sein*.[5]

Strokes of time are typically associated with clocks, raising an intriguing question about the conception of time that Heidegger attributes to Paul. What clock measures eschatological time? In the above passage, Heidegger seems to understand the event of being as a kind of clock whose strokes include the first beginning of Western philosophy with the Pre-Socratics, the various metaphysical eras from Plato to Nietzsche, and the envisaged other beginning of post-metaphysical thinking. Presumably the time measured by the clock of *beyng* is the time-space grounded by *Da-sein*. As was made clear in the previous chapter, Heidegger's notion of time-space is ultimately just another version of metaphysics. Yet if we are willing to be flexible, then we might be able to take Heidegger's idea of historical episodes as strokes of a historical clock in a more non-metaphysical and theological direction.

---

5. Heidegger, *Contributions to Philosophy*, 16.

An observation by Phillip W. Rosemann concerning Christianity and time offers a clue:

> Possessed of a definite beginning and an end, Christian time "progresses" in a sense in which Greek time cannot, it moves from creation through the Fall and the history of Israel to the Redemption of humanity through Christ and the coming of the Kingdom.[6]

Think of Jesus himself as a kind of sacred clock. The strokes of this sacred clock are the religiously significant episodes of his life, including his Incarnation, his ministry, his suffering, death, resurrection, ascension, and return at the *parousia*, which collectively constitute a single continuous movement of the Jesus-clock. In a manner comparable to how the noon movement of a standard pocket watch can be used to measure whether concomitant ordinary events transpire quickly or slowly, the designated movement of the Jesus-clock is used to measure how quickly or slowly concomitant religious events unfold. Measured against the designated movement of the Jesus-clock, Paul's lightning conversion on the road to Damascus transpires fairly quickly, whereas someone else's conversion over the course of her entire life unfolds much more slowly.

The course of concomitant ordinary events (e.g., my scribbling a note from 12:10 to 12:11, my eating a sandwich between 12:15 and 12:55) can be measured as transpiring quickly or slowly against the noon movement of the pocket watch. As the temporal standard against which the relative speed or slowness of other events occurring during its sweep are measured, the noon movement itself runs its course neither quickly nor slowly. It simply runs its course. Similarly, the movement of the Jesus clock from Incarnation to *parousia* is the *sui generis* temporal standard against which all the other concomitant Christian events in it are measured as transpiring quickly or slowly. By faith, if not by definition, the single continuous movement of the Jesus-clock is the sole temporal standard for all the other events of Christian history occurring during its sweep. There is no further clock or temporal standard against which the movement of the Jesus-clock itself runs its course quickly or slowly. It just runs. In particular, then, there is no further clock against which the course of the entire movement beginning with the Incarnation and ending in the *parousia* can be measured as unexpectedly running too slowly, as disappointingly dragging on and on. Thus the eschatological doubt that darkens the Christian present through

---

6. Rosemann, *Understanding Scholastic Thought with Foucault*, 130.

uncertainty over the sluggish "timing" of Jesus's promised future return is cleared away. Acknowledging the temporal singularity of Jesus and his life in relation to Christian time and history neither requires a metaphysical appeal to divine eternity nor implies a metaphysical conception of being as "the abyssal withholding of time-space" common to all beings.

If this deflationary analysis is incorporated into our project of developing a cogent theology of *Streit*, then two important issues still need to be addressed. The first issue is that a crucial feature Heidegger ascribes to theology has been left out. Recall once more Heidegger's "Phenomenology and Theology" view of theology as a conceptual interpretation of faith that renders faith not easier but more difficult. Clearing away a troubling eschatological paradox makes faith at least a little easier rather than more difficult. The increasing intensity and existential *frisson* that Heidegger associates with faith seem to have gone missing. Somehow, the removal of doubt-engendering difficulties must make way for more exciting ones capable of stimulating and enlivening persons of faith.

The second issue pertains to the emergence of *Da-sein*, the seeking and preserving selfhood that clears away conceptual confusions. With the clearing away of a single conceptual confusion in connection with Pauline eschatology, has *Da-sein* now emerged? It might be wondered how many actual or potential conceptual confusions about divinity must be cleared away before human beings attain *Da-sein*. We will continue to track both of these issues in the course of the present chapter.

Original Sin and the Leap into Genuine Selfhood

Another theological perplexity we encountered in chapter 2 turned on the consequences of original sin and Luther's *theologica crucis*. Luther says that through original sin, human reason has become entirely corrupt and altogether changed, depriving postlapsarian humans of their primordial being before God to the point that they are even unable to hear or answer Him without the intervention of divine grace. It is then totally unclear why original sin didn't in fact destroy prelapsarian human nature instead of only wounding it. His hostility to any application of metaphysics in theology precludes Luther from appealing to the broadly Aristotelian metaphysical explanation that original sin merely wounds human nature by removing its non-essential attributes of primordial innocence and intuitive openness to God.

The contrariety principle at the heart of Luther's *theologia crucis* initially appears to offer a non-metaphysical solution to the paradox: just as God's wisdom and power are revealed to us hidden under the folly and weakness of the Cross, the same divine wisdom and power are revealed to be at work in us hidden under our own cognitive futility and existential helplessness as we wrestle with the paradox of human nature totally destroyed by sin and subsequently redeemed by grace. Unfortunately, Luther's *theologica crucis* then seems to make suffering a permanent fixture of our relationship with God, fails to demarcate acceptable paradoxes from unacceptable ones, and leaves open the disturbing possibility that damning divine hatred is at work in us under our consternation when we confront Luther's contradiction between what *Deus incarnates et relevatus* wills and the opposite will of *Deus absconditus*.

Original sin can be accurately described as a plight in which human beings find themselves. Interestingly, Heidegger also characterizes the current human situation as "the highest plight: *the lack of a sense of plight*."[7] He elaborates on the nature of this plight:

> The lack of a sense of plight is greatest where self-certainty has become unsurpassable, where everything is held to be calculable, and especially where it has been decided, with no previous questioning who we are and what we are supposed to do. This is where the knowledge has been lost (and never was properly grounded) that genuine selfhood occurs in a grounding beyond oneself, which requires the grounding of a space and of its time.[8]

Notice how Heidegger links the human plight with the human failure to attain the genuine selfhood of seeking and preserving stewardship, or *Dasein*, that participates in the ever-expanding "grounding" or clearing work of *beyng* by removing conceptual distortions.[9] To be human is not yet to be a genuine self: "The grounding—not creating—is, from the side of *humans* (cf. the singles ones, the few . . .), a matter of letting the ground be. Thereby humans once again come to *themselves* and win back selfhood."[10]

7. Heidegger, *Contributions to Philosophy*, 85.

8. Heidegger, *Contributions to Philosophy*, 99.

9. "The most proper 'being' of humans is therefore in a belonging to the truth of being as such, and this is so, again, because the essence of being as such, not the essence of the human being, contains in itself a call to humans, as a call destining them to history (cf. The grounding, 197. *Da-sein—domain of what is proper—selfhood*)" (Heidegger, *Contributions to Philosophy*, 42).

10. Heidegger, *Contributions to Philosophy*, 27.

Does Heidegger's understanding of our plight as not only our failure to attain selfhood but also as our ignorance of our failure to do so suggest a new way of interpreting original sin that circumvents the aforementioned difficulties with Luther's view?

Echoing Kierkegaard, Heidegger stresses the need for human beings to make a "leap" (*Sprung*) into the genuine selfhood of *Da-sein*.[11] The fourth "juncture" of *Contributions* entitled "The Leap" contains passages like the following:

> Such preparedness above all requires that this truth itself already create, out of its scarcely resonating essence, the basic traits of this site (*Da-sein*). The human subject must be transformed into the builder and steward of that site.[12]

> This selfhood has to be withstood in that standing fast which allows the human being, by taking a stand in *Da-sein*, to become the being that can be encountered only in the who-question.[13]

The path to a new interpretation of original sin is beginning to take shape. *Contra* Luther, original sin is not the total corruption (destruction?) of human nature by Adam and Eve's first sins. Rather, original sin is the current inability of generically existing human beings endowed with reason and volition to become genuine human selves. In line with Heidegger's philosophical perspective in *Contributions*, becoming a self requires a leap. The trouble is that in our present condition, none of us can make the leap into selfhood.[14]

Recent work by Lisa Tessman on non-negotiable moral quandaries suggests how the notion of original sin as a plight preventing us from

---

11. Kierkegaard writes: "A human being is a synthesis of the infinite and the finite, of the temporal and the eternal, of freedom and necessity, in short, a synthesis. Considered in this way, a human being is still not a self" (Kierkegaard, *Sickness Unto Death*, 13). Further, "It is Christian heroism—a rarity, to be sure—to venture wholly to become oneself, an individual human being, alone before God, alone in this prodigious strenuousness and this prodigious responsibility" (Kierkegaard, *Sickness Unto Death*, 5). Throughout *Fear and Trembling*, Kierkegaard construes faith as a leap into genuine selfhood before God.

12. Heidegger, *Contributions to Philosophy*, 191.

13. Heidegger, *Contributions to Philosophy*, 193.

14. Heidegger's characterization of the plight as "unsurpassable" suggests this incapability, although later we will see that the philosophical situation vis-à-vis *Da-sein* is more complicated.

leaping into genuine selfhood might be fleshed out.[15] According to Tessman, an unavoidable feature of the contemporary human situation—a "plight" in which we currently find ourselves, if you will—is that we can be morally required to do something impossible. One of the numerous examples she gives is based on actual events in the aftermath of Hurricane Katrina in 2005.[16] Due to excessive flooding of New Orleans after the city's levees broke, many of the local hospitals had to be evacuated. Unfortunately, not enough rescue crews, boats, and helicopters were on hand to rescue all of the patients. Tessman asks us to imagine a Dr. Santana who is confronted with the choice between euthanizing without consent the patients who cannot be evacuated or leaving them to die a slow, agonizing, and terrifying death alone. Dr. Santana decides to administer these patients a lethal dose of drugs. Even so, she strongly feels that in doing so she commits a moral transgression. She finds herself torn between two conflicting moral requirements that she cannot jointly satisfy: not to abandon the patients, and not to kill them.[17]

Tessman contrasts negotiable moral conflicts with non-negotiable moral quandaries. In a negotiable moral conflict, the agent can decide through a reasoning process to override one of the conflicting moral requirements and then either substitute or compensate for it. A teacher who must choose between keeping her appointment to meet with a student before a test or taking her sick cat to the vet may decide to override the first requirement and then substitute something else for it, such as meeting with the student later in the day.[18] Even if overriding a requirement results in an irreplaceable loss, as when the teacher's decision to stay with the sick cat deprives her student of the teacher's professional aid before Friday's test, some irreplaceable losses may be taken in stride and compensated for with a lesser value, as when the teacher arranges to have her non-professional

---

15. Although Tessman's concerns are non-theological, there is no reason in principle why theology cannot profit from some of her insights.

16. See Tessman, *When Doing the Right Thing Is Impossible*, 1–17.

17. Tessman also describes moral quandaries where there is only a single moral requirement that someone cannot satisfy. She gives the example of a father whose disabled child continues to be badly bullied at school despite the fact that the father has done everything within his power to protect his child from bullying. The father strongly feels that he has failed to meet the single moral requirement of protecting his vulnerable child from bullying. See Tessman, *When Doing the Right Thing Is Impossible*, 20.

18. See Tessman, *When Doing the Right Thing Is Impossible*, 48–50.

graduate assistant meet with the student on Thursday.[19] Since in a negotiable moral conflict something can either substitute or compensate for not fulfilling the overridden moral requirement, the latter is cancelled so that the agent commits no wrongdoing by not fulfilling it.

However, Tessman argues, in a non-negotiable moral quandary nothing can substitute or compensate for the irreplaceable loss that results from not fulfilling an overridden moral requirement. When Dr. Santana decides to euthanize the patients who cannot be evacuated and thus to fulfill the moral requirement of not abandoning them, nothing can substitute or compensate for her not fulfilling the overridden moral requirement to avoid killing them without consent. Or if instead she had decided to leave the patients behind and thus to fulfill the moral requirement of not killing them without consent, then nothing could have compensated for her not fulfilling the overridden moral requirement to avoid abandoning them to an agonizing death.[20] Since nothing can substitute or compensate for not fulfilling the overridden moral requirement, Dr. Santana commits a moral wrong by not fulfilling it, though she is not morally blameworthy as long as her own choices did not contribute to the untenable situation in which she finds herself.[21] Yet whatever course of action Dr. Santana decides to pursue, she will commit a moral transgression. The same is true for anyone else confronted with a non-negotiable moral quandary.[22] Unavoidably and inevitably they will fail morally.

In order to relate Tessman's analysis to the issue of original sin, suppose that we human beings who are generically endowed with reason and

19. See Tessman, *When Doing the Right Thing Is Impossible*, 54–58, for her discussion of irreplaceable losses to be taken in stride.

20. Similarly, nothing substitutes or compensates for the irreplaceable loss resulting from the father's not fulfilling the single moral requirement to protect his disabled and vulnerable child from all bullying.

21. For the difference between committing a moral wrong and being morally blameworthy for doing so see Tessman, *When Doing the Right Thing Is Impossible*, 159

22. As Tessman plausibly observes, there is something amiss with trying to justify the moral requirements operative in non-negotiable moral quandaries through a reasoning process. Rather, we judge ourselves to be bound by these requirements through an automatic intuitive process. For more details, see Tessman, *When Doing the Right Thing Is Impossible*, 105–111. Tessman also emphasizes how our practice of making moral judgments is risky, since we may come to see that something we initially regarded as an intuitively binding moral requirement is actually a product of problematic assumptions about race, gender, or sexuality. See Tessman, *When Doing the Right Thing Is Impossible*, 142, 156.

volition want to make the leap to a particular kind of individuality we might call *being a perfectly ethical self*. A perfectly ethical self is someone who actually fulfills every moral requirement in any actual situation she encounters and is also capable of fulfilling every moral requirement in any conceivable situation in which she might find herself. Each perfectly ethical self is distinguished from the others through the series of actual situations unique to her own life in which she actually fulfills every moral requirement. Such impeccable moral uprightness is not something accidental or extraneous to a perfectly ethical self but stems from his or her own capability to fulfill every moral requirement in any conceivable situation. Being a perfectly ethical self means being the morally best person it is possible for you to be—a highly admirable identity that anyone who has not yet become a genuine self might reasonably wish to acquire. Especially if a perfectly good God exists whom we love and wish to emulate as much as possible, wanting to become a perfectly ethical self makes perfectly good sense.[23]

What Tessman's analysis of non-negotiable moral quandaries reveals is that no one can ever make the leap to this kind of selfhood. At some point in the course of our lives, we may very well find ourselves confronted with a moral quandary in which there is some moral requirement we should but cannot fulfill. Even if we somehow never land in an actual moral quandary, there are conceivable situations in which we could not fulfill all of the binding moral requirements. The fact that we manage to avoid any of these quandaries is merely a matter of our good fortune rather than our goodness, as Milton reminds us:

> I cannot praise a fugitive and cloistered virtue, unexercised and unbreathed, that never sallies out and sees her adversary but slinks out of the race, where that immortal garland is to be run for, not without dust and heat.[24]

Original sin, then, is our plight that there always will or could be situations in which we commit a moral wrong because we cannot fulfill a moral requirement we are obliged to fulfill. We are not morally blameworthy for this plight, which may have arisen through the bad choices of previous humans. Nevertheless, we can never make the leap to perfectly ethical selfhood.

There can be no moral quandaries without a plurality of non-negotiable moral requirements, norms, or values. Tessman tells a particular story

23. Jesus instructs his disciples, "So be perfect, just as your heavenly Father is perfect" (Matt 5:48).

24. Milton, *Areopagitica*, 13.

about the genesis of moral values. She claims that although the ultimate cause of cooperation in human groups is natural selection, there are many proximate causes of social cooperation. Proximate causes of cooperation include empathy, fear of punishment, hope of earning a good reputation, anticipation of feeling good about oneself, and many others.[25] Some proximate causes of social cooperation are specifically moral. How does a proximate cause of cooperation become a value possessing moral authority? Tessman answers:

> People are socialized to consider these traits and practices to be morally good, or morally required. When this happens, we can say that these proximate causes of cooperation have been *moralized*— that is, members of the society have imbued them with a special sort of authority that they will understand to be moral authority.[26]

Perhaps influenced by Nietzsche, Heidegger is extremely skeptical about "the remaining caught up in the thinking and establishing of 'values' and 'ideas' . . . without any serious questioning."[27] He might argue that the very idea of moral values needs to be deflated before the leap to *Da-sein* can be accomplished. Why?

With Tessman, Heidegger would reject as a metaphysical illusion the notion of moral values existing independently of us. If there is any such thing as morality, then it is something we ourselves construct.[28] The question is exactly how the process of constructing moral values is supposed to work. From Tessman's description, what makes some proximate cause of cooperation a moral value is that we decide to keep *imbuing* it with moral authority: "To be counted as a morally valuable trait, we—some moral community—must actually value it in a certain way: we must have imbued it, and continue to imbue it, with moral authority."[29] This description is unsatisfactory.

To see to why, imagine that a grove of trees is a proximate cause of social cooperation, in that the beauty of the trees prompts a community to tend them. The people in the community then imbue the grove with divinity, to the point that it becomes unthinkable for them that the trees are anything other than gods. Yet if the sole reason why the trees seem to be

25. See Tessman, *When Doing the Right Thing is Impossible*, 84–85.

26. Tessman, *Where Doing the Right Thing Is Impossible*, 86.

27. Heidegger, *Contributions to Philosophy*, 93.

28. See Tessman, *Where Doing the Right Thing Is Impossible*, 142–43.

29. Tessman, *When Doing the Right Thing Is Impossible*, 88.

gods is that the people have treated and continue to treat the trees as gods, then as soon as the people come to realize this fact it is hard to fathom how they could continue to regard the trees as having genuine sacred authority. For the idea of the trees as gods is nothing more than a communal fabrication, a story the people have made up and keep telling themselves. It is similarly difficult to fathom how we can continue to regard some trait as a moral value as soon as we come to realize that the sole reason why the trait seems to be so is our ongoing decision to keep treating it as such. As Nietzsche urges, like gods, moral values are nothing more than put-up jobs, entrenched projections we have made and continue to make.[30] Recognizing them for the collective fictions they are, we can opt out of them if we resolve to do so.[31] Once the conceptual confusion of "moral values" is discarded, then there are also no such things as perfectly ethical selfhood or non-negotiable moral quandaries that prevent us from attaining it. Instead, the way is now clear for human beings to leap into non-metaphysical and non-moral selfhood: the seeking and preserving stewardship of *Da-sein*. Or so the Heidegger of *Contributions* might argue.

A concern mooted earlier in the current chapter continues to haunt the clearing work that Heidegger associates with *Da-sein*. Even after Heidegger's potentially confusing assignment-consignment rhetoric has been set jettisoned, it remains the case no matter how many metaphysical or other philosophical misconceptions we have cleared away, we could have always done so more skillfully and we could always clear away new confusions. Without a determinate threshold of deflationary success, we may doubt whether we have actually leaped into the seeking and preserving stewardship constituting the selfhood of *Da-sein*.[32] Heidegger provides

30. For example: "Only after we have once recognized that everything consists of lies and appearance, shall we have earned the right to uphold this most beautiful of all fictions—virtue" (Nietzsche, *Will to Power*, 157). It is merely because we continue to uphold the "lie" or fiction of moral values that they possess any semblance of authority over us.

31. Worse, Tessman's account of the origin of moral values flirts with vicious circularity: no traits can become binding moral values unless some moral community imbues them with moral authority. But presumably, no community can be moral unless it is already bound by moral values. Hence the genesis of any moral values presupposes that there already are moral values.

32. Doubt about *Da-sein* is structurally parallel to a kind of doubt engendered by Kierkegaard's leap of faith. Abraham passes the test of faith through his willingness to sacrifice Isaac in obedience to God's command while still believing that God will somehow restore Isaac to him. Few of us have ever been tested in this way. How do we know whether we would pass the test if someday we were? And even if I have been tested in this

no philosophical remedy for such doubt. However, as we have seen, his reference to the strife between the god and the human being does suggest a theological remedy. We have leaped into *Da-sein* once our work of clearing away misconceptions places us in the position to make a decision that results in the absconding or the appearing of the last god. Whether we could have done better or done more in rooting out conceptual confusions is irrelevant as long as we have done enough in order to reach this decision. Have we?

HAVING TO DECIDE WITHOUT KNOWING HOW

In chapter 3 it was argued that the purported intentional correlate of the methodologically key experience of anxiety is an uncanny divinity distinct from each of the five ontological conditions countenanced by Heidegger's phenomenology: being an individual human thrown into the world (*Dasein* as analyzed in *Sein und Zeit*), being a particular non-human entity in the world (e.g., a jug, a tree, or a spider), the totality of beings in the world (*die Seiende*), the non-metaphysical event of *beyng* (*das Ereignis*), and total nothingness (*das Nichts*). At various places in his writings, Heidegger describes how each ontological condition can prompt us to experience anxiety in the face of something uncanny. If this uncanny something were simply identical with any one of these conditions, then we would have an experience of the uncanny only when we are confronted with the condition in question, never when we are confronted with any of the other conditions. Since we do also sometimes experience the other conditions as uncanny, it follows that the uncanny transcends all of them. As transcendent, the uncanny otherness is divine.

We wondered exactly why divinity strikes us as uncanny, and why the ontological conditions prompt us to feel anxious about it. Heidegger's stress in the *Contributions* on the necessity of making a decision concerning the last god now enables us to answer both questions. To make the leap to *Da-sein* as seeking and preserving stewardship, we must decide in such a way that the last god will powerfully "pass by" us. Yet all we are given to go on in making this decision are the five ontological conditions that are described by Heidegger. Divinity in the guise of the last god strikes us

---

way, how do I know whether I would pass another such test should God decide to submit me to it? How does Abraham himself know whether he would? Our uncertainty about these questions may lead us to doubt whether we really have faith.

as uncanny because even after we have exhausted these ontological conditions, we still have not encountered the last god. This deity seems forever beyond our reach, impossibly remote. The ontological conditions prompt us to feel anxious about divinity because we are still somehow supposed to make a fateful decision resulting in the last god's theophany. It is as if we were responsible for finding an especially rare and precious jewel in a house full of what we know are empty rooms.

Thus Heidegger leaves us in the theological predicament of having to make a fateful decision about the last god that we have no idea how to make. The last god does not appear to us through our reflection on individual human existence or on any particular non-human being, through our contemplation of the totality of beings, through our participation in the non-metaphysical event of appropriation, or through our meditation on utter nothingness, since the last god is none of the previous conditions. Nonetheless, we bear the responsibility for whether the last god appears or never appears to us as a consequence of our decision. From a Heideggerian perspective, original sin is not the moral plight that we are incapable of becoming perfectly ethical selves, but the religious plight that nothing phenomenologically accessible to us enables us to become genuinely devout selves who are vividly aware of their God. The next three chapters will take up the issue of whether Heidegger hints at any possible path(s) out of this thicket.

Chapter 6

Divine Intimacy through Divine Remoteness

I look for it, but there are always
distractions—eleven magpies cawing, rocking,
crowded in one small-boned locust tree.

I search, but my concentration
is broken by the pattern of leaf shadows
moving on the wall, the fragrances of pine sugar,
sage, dry red grasses in the air.

I say prayers, but the evening thunder,
the gully wind . . . I have to stop
and check the sky.[1]

APOPHATIC HINTS

THE POETIC LINES JUST quoted echo the peculiar theological predicament that surfaces in Heidegger's *Beiträge zur Philosophie*. We feel ourselves charged with the responsibility of undergoing a theophany, a powerful experience of the holy that Heidegger calls "the passing by of the last god."[2]

1. Rogers, "Why Divinity Remains Lost," 518–19.
2. "I try to meditate. I try to set my mind firmly on the task" (Rogers, "Why Divinity Remains Lost," 519).

So we ardently search for signs of this mysterious divinity. Yet no matter where we look, we cannot find it. Even after we have exhausted all the possible phenomena available to us, the god in question still does not appear. What have we done wrong? What could we have done differently? Pausing to check the sky once again, we are gripped by the anxiety of being required to do something we have no idea how to do.

However, within the same poem there is a tantalizing ambivalence:

> Again, just devils
> I suppose—the night that is nothing
> soothing around my face, my hair,
> the stars, seeded by an uneven hand,
> so profuse, so demanding, so clearly
> insistent in their silence.[3]

For the breath of an instant, it is as if the deity is powerfully present to us in the very signs that initially seemed to announce its remoteness from us: the magpies, the leaf shadows moving on the wall, the natural fragrances, the thunder, the gully wind, and the night that is nothing soothing the hair around my face and scattered with stars. As another poet whom Heidegger quotes says,

> Was ist Gott? unbekannt, dennoch
> Voll Eigenschaften ist das Angesicht
> Des Himmels von ihm.

> What is God? Unknown, and yet
> Full of qualities is the face
> Of heaven with him.[4]

Perhaps the way out of the theological predicament Heidegger leaves us in lies in our recognition that the last god paradoxically draws near to us through its remoteness and our inability to decide about it. Apophatically, the last god might be passing us by precisely when we take it *not* to be passing us by.

The present chapter carefully weighs whether this suggestion can be expanded into cogent proposal for overcoming the Heideggerian theological

---

3. Rogers, "Why Divinity Remains Lost," 519.

4. Hölderlin, "Was ist Gott," 270–71. For Heidegger's discussion of these lines, see Heidegger, "Poetically Man Dwells," 225.

predicament. At various places in the *Beiträge*, Heidegger's rhetoric of the last god's nearness-in-remoteness sows the seeds for such a proposal. It has obvious affinities with Luther's contrariety principle. We will also see how the divine nearness-in-remoteness (DNR) proposal promises to avoid the problems we described with Luther's *theoligia crucis* by identifying nearness-in-remoteness with specific, highly positive phenomena entirely different from the negative affectivities of eschatological affliction or cognitive consternation before unfathomable contradiction. Unfortunately, the only examples of nearness-in-remoteness phenomena that Heidegger gives are either spatial or temporal. Since the last god is distinct from space or time, it remains obscure how any positive experience of nearness in farness applies to divinity *per se*. It is concluded that the DNR proposal ultimately renders the idea of the holy wholly empty.

A Promising Gambit

Early in the *Beiträge*, Heidegger applies the nearness-remoteness motif to divinity:

> Nearness to the last god is reticence, which must be set into work and word in the style of restraint. *To be* in the nearness of the god—even if this nearness is the most remote remoteness of the undecidability regarding the absconding or advent of the gods—cannot be calculated in terms of "good fortune" or "misfortune."[5]

> At the "disposal of the gods" means to stand far away and outside—i.e., outside the common way of understanding and interpreting "beings"—and to belong to the most distant ones, those to whom the absconding of the gods in the gods' farthest withdrawal is what is closest.[6]

Even in the contemporary plight where we generic human beings are mired in metaphysical confusion and have not yet made the leap into the genuine selfhood of *Da-sein*, divinity manifested both in singularity ("the last god") and plurality ("the gods") is paradoxically near to us through its very remoteness.[7]

5. Heidegger, *Contributions to Philosophy*, 12.

6. Heidegger, *Contributions to Philosophy*, 17.

7. Heidegger's insistence that "*Da-sein* does not count gods (Heidegger, *Contributions to Philosophy*, 231) and that "the multiplicity of gods is not subject to enumeration

Heidegger underscores how "The last god is not the event itself and yet is in need of the event as that to which the one who grounds the 'there' belongs."[8] For the last god to appear, obviously it must appear to someone. On the reading of the *Beiträge* advanced in the previous chapter, the someone in question is *Da-sein*, the style of seeking and preserving stewardship that begins to emerge as human beings participate in the clearing event of ferreting out conceptual confusions that skew their understanding of divinity. Thus the last god needs the clearing event to which the "there" of *Da-sein* belongs, similar to how a successful performance requires an appreciative audience. Equally, however, full-blown *Da-sein* as devout selfhood before vividly experienced divinity also requires the appearing of the last god. Between the last god and full-blown *Da-sein*, then, there is a reciprocity that Heidegger seems to think somehow unfolds through the last god's paradoxical nearness-in-remoteness:

> The greatest nearness of the last god eventuates when the event, as the hesitant self-withholding, is elevated into *refusal*. The extreme remoteness of the last god in the refusal is a peculiar nearness, a relation that must not be deformed by "dialectics."[9]

What is needed in order to transform Heidegger's suggestive remarks about divine nearness-in-remoteness into a definite proposal is an explanation of the "how" in this "somehow."

If not an explanation, then at least the intimation of one can be found in passages where Heidegger begins to probe the phenomenology of what he calls "trembling":

> *Beyng* is the trembling of this divinization [in which the gods first divinize and bring their god into a decision], trembling as the expanding of the temporal-spatial playing field in which the

---

but, instead, to the inner richness of the grounds and abysses in the site of the moment of the lighting up and concealment of the last god" (Heidegger, *Contributions to Philosophy*, 326) discourages any polytheistic interpretation of divinity in the *Beiträge*; rather, the richness of this divinity encompasses both singularity and plurality. The latter thought is not uncongenial to the one God in three Persons professed in Christianity. Chapters 7 and 8 will return to the issue of whether a non-metaphysical construal of the Trinity is possible within the *Streit* theology we seek to develop.

8. Heidegger, *Contributions to Philosophy*, 324.

9. Heidegger, *Contributions to Philosophy*, 326. "Dialectics" is presumably a swipe at Hegel's metaphysical conception of being as Absolute Spirit punctuated by the dialectic of thesis, antithesis, and synthesis.

trembling itself, as refusal, appropriates to itself its clearing (the "there").[10]

Like Heidegger's notion of a leap, the notion of trembling (*Zittern*) evokes Kierkegaardian fear and trembling (*Furcht und Zittern*). Only now, trembling is not apprehension before the counterintuitive commands of an inscrutable deity but rising excitement among those involved in the non-metaphysical event of appropriation as what initially appears to be the total absence of the last god becomes pervaded with its breathtaking nearness:

> The trembling of the coming to be of the oscillation, the appropriation of the belonging, grounding, sheltering *Da-sein* to the intimation—this essential occurrence of *beyng* is not itself the last god; instead, the essential occurrence of being grounds the sheltering, and thereby the creative preservation, of the god, who *pervades beyng* with *divinity* always only in work and sacrifice, deed and thought. Hence thinking, as inaugural of the other beginning, also may come into the remote nearness of the last god.[11]

Far from merely chanting the phrase "the remote nearness of the last god" as yet another in long line of apophatic mantras in the history of *via negative theology*, Heidegger is associating the remote nearness of the last god with a quite definite and extraordinarily affirmative experience of trembling excitement. The potential repercussions for our own theological project are significant.

The Heideggerian idea of divine nearness revealed through divine remoteness is reminiscent of the Lutheran idea of God's power, wisdom, and other divine attributes revealed as hidden under their contrary forms of human weakness, foolishness, cognitive futility, and existential helplessness. A crucial difference is that, unlike Luther, Heidegger associates our encountering divine nearness-in-remoteness with our undergoing an intensely passionate form of *positive* affectivity. Doing so would enable Heidegger to evade the three difficulties we described that threaten to undermine Luther's *theologia crucis*. Suppose that we finally become full-blown *Da-sein* by experiencing the last god's remote nearness in trembling excitement, forming "the net in which the last god is suspended in order to rend the net and let it end in its uniqueness, divine and rare and the strangest

10. Heidegger, *Contributions to Philosophy*, 192.

11. Heidegger, *Contributions to Philosophy*, 206. Heidegger's use of "Dasein" in the passage has been changed to "*Da-sein*," since the reference to creative preservation makes it clear that Heidegger has in view *Da-sein* as seeking and preserving stewardship.

among all beings."[12] For Heidegger, this ultimate theophany comes closest to what traditional theology conceives as blessed humans dwelling in endless beatitude with God in heaven. As trembling excitement, it is free from distress, torment, or any other kind of negative affectivity that Luther risks making a permanent fixture of *any* human relationship with God—even a "heavenly" one. Furthermore, although divine nearness-in-remoteness is certainly paradoxical, if it is associated with a quite definite human experience of trembling excitement then it can be sharply demarcated from unacceptable paradoxes or absurdities like round squares or from patent contradictions like a deity who wills both that no sinners and that some sinners are predestined to damnation. Thus the thrilling paradox of the last god's remote nearness is worlds apart from the numbing anguish engendered by Luther's dialectic between *Deus incarnates et revelatus* and *Deus absconditus*.

Our task now is to zero in on the phenomenology of Heideggerian trembling. The *noesis-noema* distinction first mentioned in chapter 3 equips us with a useful tool. The noetic pole of the intentional experience of trembling is intense excitement, a feeling with which we are all familiar. Yet the same experience's noematic pole, that about which we are intensely excited, is not a new romantic relationship or a fascinating job opportunity or a cliffhanger at the sports stadium. It is nearness-in-remoteness. What situations or contexts does Heidegger describe that give us a purchase on this particular noema? In order to find them, we must look beyond the *Beiträge* and consult other texts where he takes up the theme of remote nearness.

Spatial and Temporal Nearness-in-Remoteness

In "Building Dwelling Thinking," Heidegger begins to bring nearness-in-remoteness down to earth with a concrete example:

12. Heidegger, *Contributions to Philosophy*, 207. The *Streit* theologian will caution against any interpretation of this passage according to which the last god is the strangest *being* amid all beings, since the last god is not any particular being. (If "it" is instead taken to refer to the net in which the last god is suspended then the net should also not be interpreted as the strangest being, since the net is said to be the same as the appropriating event where the latter is also not any particular being.) Presumably, something that is strangest of all could come to pass amid all the instances of a given ontological category without being any one of them; e.g., strangest of all amid all nations on the earth would the achievement of lasting peace, even though lasting peace itself is not a nation.

> If all of us now think, from right where we are, of the old bridge in
> Heidelberg, this thinking toward that location is not a mere expe-
> rience inside the persons present here; rather, it belongs to the na-
> ture of thinking *of* that bridge that *in itself* thinking gets through,
> persists through, the distance to that location. From this spot right
> here, we are there are the bridge—we are by no means at some
> representational content in our consciousness. *From right here we*
> *may even be much nearer to that bridge and to what it makes room*
> *for than someone who uses it daily as an indifferent river crossing.*[13]

The noema of the thinking experience Heidegger calls to mind is the old
bridge in Heidelberg. Even though we are many miles away from it, the
bridge might be nearer to us as an emotional concern or a theme for philosophical reflection than it is to people who walk across the bridge every day
without giving it any thought. Phenomenologically, our experience of the
bridge is also different from the experience of someone who becomes aware
of the bridge while standing on or under it, since it is part of our experience
but not part of hers that the bridge is spatially distant.

In another text, Heidegger ups the ante by observing how we can experience nearness-in-spatial remoteness itself:

> Two isolated farmsteads—if any such are left—separated by an
> hour's walk across the fields, can be the best of neighbors, while
> two townhouses, facing each other across the street or even shar-
> ing a common wall, know no neighborhood. . . . Goethe, and
> Mörike too, like to use the phrase "face-to-face with one another"
> not only with respect to human beings but also with respect to
> things of the world. Where this prevails, all things are open to one
> another in their self-concealment; thus one extends itself to the
> other, and thus all remain themselves; one is over the other as its
> guardian watching over the other, over it as its veil.[14]

Here, the noematic focus is not the two farmsteads themselves but the
neighborly nearness they share despite being spatially far apart. Other
things separated by a considerable spatial distance—the brook behind the
first farmstead and the lane passing by the second farmstead, the fields
between the farmsteads and the stars twinkling high above in the night
sky—all draw closer to one other as belonging to this same neighborhood,
a phenomenon that Heidegger calls "nighness" (*Nahheit*).

13. Heidegger, "Building Dwelling Thinking," 156–57 (final emphasis added).
14. Heidegger, "Nature of Language," 103–4.

Heidegger's description of the isolated farmsteads' mutual remoteness as an hour's walk across the fields implies that nearness-in-remoteness can also be experienced temporally. The theme reappears in a passage from a very late work:

> This nearing of nearness keeps open the approach coming from the future by withholding the present in the approach. Nearing nearness has the character of denial and withholding. It unifies in advance the ways in which what has-been, what is about to be, and the present reach out toward each other.[15]

Admittedly, in the same work, Heidegger goes on to equate nearing nearness with the temporal aspect of time-space as abyssal self-withholding[16]—a speculative turn that, as we saw in chapter 4, reinstates metaphysics by treating temporal-spatial self-withholding as a maximally general characteristic common to all beings.

But instead of reading the above passage as introducing a new metaphysics of time-space, we may interpret it non-metaphysically as gesturing toward a particular experience of time. Sometimes, something that happened many years ago or something that will happen tomorrow might be more present to us than what is happening right now. Occasionally, this experience of temporal displacement spills over onto the temporal dimensions themselves itself, as when William Faulkner gives voice to the quintessentially Southern experience that "The past is never dead. It's not even past,"[17] or when the novelist Leonardo Sciascia eloquently articulates the brooding fatalism endemic to his fellow Sicilians:

> We ignore the future tense of verbs. We never say, "Tomorrow I will go to the country"; we say, "*Dumani, vaju in compagna*"— "Tomorrow I am going to the country." How can you fail to be pessimistic in a country where the future tense of the verb does not exist?[18]

It could even be argued that the phenomenological idiosyncrasy of both spatial nearness-in-remoteness and temporal nearness-in-remoteness militates against treating them as maximally general characteristics common to all beings, since the relevant experiences are in fact uncommonly rare.

---

15. Heidegger, "Time and Being," 15–16.

16. See especially Heidegger, "Time and Being," 22.

17. Faulkner, *Requiem for a Nun*, 73.

18. Sciascia, *La Sicile comme métaphore*, 53, quoted in Kelly, *Great Mortality*, 83.

Yet are the relevant experiences of spatial and temporal nearness-in-remoteness *too* rare? What, if any, relation obtains between them and the nearness-in-remoteness of the last god?

MAKING THE HOLY WHOLLY EMPTY

In evaluating the DNR proposal, the first observation to be made is that on those rare occasions when we experience spatial or temporal nearness-in-remoteness, we are not experiencing the last god. For the last god cannot be the same as any of the spatiotemporal phenomena described in the previous section. The reason is clear from the primary argument given in chapter 3, according to which uncanny divinity is distinct from any of the five ontological conditions (individual human existence or *Da-sein* as Heidegger understands it in *Sein und Zeit*, any specific non-human being, *die Seiende*, *Ereignis*, or *das Nichts*) countenanced by Heidegger. In particular, then, the uncanny divinity that supposedly draws near to us through its very remoteness is not the same as the non-metaphysical event of appropriation, which includes spatiotemporal nearness-in-remoteness, or *Nahheit*. Hence it is far from obvious how our vivid experiences of the latter can translate into an encounter with the last god's remote nearness.

An advocate of the DNR proposal might reply that *that* is exactly the point. Nothing could be further from divinity than whatever is wholly other than it; ontological distinctness is remoteness *par excellence*. Hence as an uncanny something that is ontologically distinct from any individualized human existence, any particular non-human being, the totality of beings, the non-metaphysical event of *beyng* structured by spatiotemporal *Nahheit*, and the possibility absolute nothingness, the last god is maximally remote from all of these phenomena and thus from us as we are anxiously experiencing them. Paradoxically, the last god's intimate nearness consists in its maximal remoteness via its ontological distinctness from us and anything else—or so someone sympathetic to the proposal under consideration might say.

Prima facie, the foregoing reply on behalf of the DNR proposal is confronted by an obvious difficulty. In general, the ontological distinctness of X from Y does not guarantee the maximal remoteness of X from Y, let alone that X is intimately near to Y through X's maximal remoteness from Y. Returning to one of Heidegger's examples, two townhouses facing each other across the street or even sharing a common wall are ontologically distinct from each other. Yet as Heidegger himself points out, the two townhouses do not share *Nahheit* or any other kind of remote nearness. Perhaps two or more phenomena, such as the farmsteads separated by an hour's walk across the fields, cannot share *Nahheit* unless they are ontologically distinct from one another. But then ontological distinctness is at best a necessary rather than a sufficient condition for remote nearness.

There is one last twist to consider. A defender of the DNR proposal might grant that while ontological distinctness is not generally a sufficient condition for nearness-in-remoteness, the exception to the rule is divinity. Solely in the case where X is the last god does the mere ontological distinctness of X from Y guarantee X's intimate nearness to Y through X's maximal remoteness from Y. That is just what we should expect, the defender of the proposal might urge, given the last god's uncanny and *sui generis* status. Nothing else like it is even conceivable. If so, then in order to draw near to us through its remoteness, the last god does not have to be spatiotemporal. It only has to be ontologically distinct from us, which it certainly is in light of the fact that the last god is not the same as any particular human being. Since the last god is also not the same as any particular non-human being, the totality of beings, the non-metaphysical event of *beyng*, or total nonbeing, it is also intimately near to each one of these ontological conditions.

But then what becomes of the extraordinarily powerful and positive experience of oscillation, the trembling excitement we are supposed to feel upon encountering the last god's paradoxical remote nearness? Instead of a net in which the last god is vividly suspended before us in all its uniqueness, rareness, and strangeness, the experience in question is now a net that has been cast so wide as to cover everything and thus to capture nothing. This cul-de-sac is already implied by the considerable flexibility with which Heidegger applies the nearness-in-remoteness trope across various situations. Whether we are in a plight marked by pervasive metaphysical confusion and generic humanity, or a transitional phase where the genuine selfhood of *Da-sein* as seeking and preserving stewardship is beginning to emerge even though we have not yet decided about divinity, or a moment where the decision has been made and blazing divinity gloriously irradiates the entire temporal-spatial playing field of full-blown *Da-sein*, the last god is ontologically distinct from us and hence—at least according to the envisaged defense of the DNR proposal—intimately near to us through its remoteness from us. The phenomenological common denominator of all these situations is zero: a "trembling excitement" that cuts across all the

foregoing scenarios is neither trembling nor exciting but something so ano-
dyne as to be unnoticeable.

Early in *An Introduction to Metaphysics*, Heidegger quotes an evoca-
tive passage from the Norwegian writer Knut Hamsun's novel *The Road
Leads On* where the main character, August, is spending his last days alone
in the mountains:

> Here he sits between his ears and all he hears is emptiness. An
> amusing conception, indeed. On the sea there were both motion
> and sound, something for the ear to feed on, a chorus of waters.
> Here nothingness meets nothingness and the result is zero, not
> even a hole. Enough to make one shake one's head, utterly at a
> loss.[19]

Ultimately, the divine nearness-in-remoteness proposal dead-ends in the
same kind of emptiness August feels. A last god who is equally near to us
and to everything else no matter what we say, think, or do is not an exciting advent of the holy that galvanizes us by passing us by but a complete
irrelevance. We must search elsewhere if we are to take the next step on the
path of *Streit* theology.

19. Hamsun, *Road Leads On*, 508, quoted by Heidegger in *Introduction to Metaphysics*, 27.

Chapter 7

God as Essential Nothingness

In January 1976 Heidegger requested that his Messkirch compatriot, the Freiburg professor of theology Bernhard Welte, visit him for a talk. He informed him that, when the time came, he would like to be buried in the Messkirch cemetery. This last conversation between the two men centered on the experience that proximity to death included within itself proximity to one's native soil. "Floating in the room," Welte reported, "was also Eckhart's idea that God equaled Nothingness."[1]

ONCE UPON A JUG

THE ELUSIVE DIVINITY DESCRIBED in Heidegger's *Beiträge*—the enigmatic last god whose appearing or absconding fatefully depends on our making a decision that so far we have no clue how to make—is not the same as the ontological condition of total nonbeing where there are no non-human beings, no human beings (whether or not they have attained *Da-sein*) and no event of *beyng* (whether it occurs in a distorted, metaphysical manner or in a non-distorted, non-metaphysical way). Hence if Eckhart's equation between God and nothingness is to be taken seriously, there must be more to nothingness than total ontological negation. Does Heidegger say anything that tends in this direction?

---

1. Safranski, *Martin Heidegger*, 432. The quotation is taken from Welte, "Erinnerung an ein spätes Gespräch," 251.

Already in the *Beiträge*, Heidegger takes pains to differentiate between nothingness proper and mere nonbeing as the total ontological negation he regards as the goal of nihilism:

> Accordingly, [in the entire history of metaphysics] nothingness is always grasped as a nonbeing and thus as *negativum*. If "nothingness" in this sense is even posited as a goal, then "pessimistic nihilism" is consummated, the disdain for every effete "philosophy of nothingness" [like, presumably, Heidegger's] is legitimated, and, above all, one is exempted from any questioning, while the "heroic thinkers" are distinguished precisely by their promoting this exemption. There is not the least in common between all this and my questioning of nothingness, which arises out of the question of the truth of *beyng*. Nothingness is neither negative nor a "goal." Instead, it is the essential trembling of *beyng* itself and therefore *is* more than any being.[2]

Not only has Western metaphysics misconstrued *beyng* as the maximally general characteristic common to all beings, it has also distorted essential nothingness or *nonbeying* by reducing it to mere nonbeing: "But *nonbeing* essentially occurs, and *beyng* essentially occurs; *nonbeing essentially occurs in the distorted essence, beyng essentially occurs as permeated with negativity.*"[3]

Theologically, these passages from the *Beiträge* contain several potentially interesting leads. One is that *nonbeying* or essential nothingness, though certainly not a being, is not purely negative but also possesses positive features. Another is that essential nothingness as the trembling of *beyng* is intimately related to the non-metaphysical event. Yet trembling can also be identified with *Da-sein*'s excitement before the passing by of revealed divinity. Additionally, what in chapter 4 we called the clearing work of *beyng* that is necessary but not sufficient for the emergence of full-blown *Da-sein* includes our realization of the world's radical contingency, since there might not have been anything at all. Perhaps essential nothingness is a plausible candidate for a Heideggerian divinity that encompasses the non-metaphysical event sheltered in beings by full-blown *Da-sein* and total ontological negation as distinct possibilities without being reducible to any one of them. If so, then further meditation on essential nothingness could

2. Heidegger, *Contributions to Philosophy*, 209.
3. Heidegger, *Contributions to Philosophy*, 210.

aid us in making a decision that will result in the last god's appearing instead of absconding.

So far, the leads we have mentioned are all rather abstract. To begin fleshing them out, something else Heidegger says in the *Beiträge* is relevant:

> Yet the open realm, which conceals itself at the same time that beings come to stand in it in each case (indeed not only the things most proximately at hand), is in fact something like an *inner recess* [*hohle Mitte*], e.g., that of a jug. Yet it must be realized that the inner recess is not just a haphazard emptiness which arises purely on account of the surrounding walls and which happens not to be full of "things." It is just the opposite: the inner recess itself is what determines, shapes, and bears the walling action of the walls and of their surfaces. The walls and surfaces are merely what is radiated out by the original open realm which allows its openness to come into play by summoning up, round about itself and toward itself, such-and-such walls (the particular form of the vessel).[4]

What is intriguing about Heidegger's description of the jug is how its inner recess functions as a positive nullity that creates the vessel by allowing the sides and their base to gather around itself. Moreover, the inner recess is said to be an open realm creatively at work in other cases where beings come to stand around or in it. The fact that God is traditionally understood as the Creator already suggests that the Heideggerian idea of essential nothingness or emptiness might be theologically fruitful.

Initially, it is. A closer look at Heidegger's phenomenology of hollowness reveals how essential emptiness exceeds total ontological negation by playing what may be described as creative, delineative, and captivating roles familiar to us from our own experience. Indeed, essential emptiness sometimes plays all three roles simultaneously, opening the door at least a crack to a Heideggerian model of divine Trinity in unity. What we then have is not a God of the gaps but a God who is these very gaps in their tripartite activity, as it were. Since our experiential encounter with creative, delineative, and captivating emptiness can be deeply purposeful and fulfilling rather than *Angst*-ridden, identifying the last god with triune essential emptiness seems to offer us a way of interacting positively and decisively with divinity. Let us call this the divinity as essential nothingness (DEN) proposal for overcoming the theological predicament of having to decide about the last god without knowing how to decide.

---

4. Heidegger, *Contributions to Philosophy*, 268.

The sticking point for the DEN proposal concerns the nature of modality. It will be argued that no plausible explanation of how possibility and necessity relate to God as essential nothingness and the non-metaphysical event of being can be extracted from Heidegger's own ambiguous statements in the *Beiträge*. Sometimes Heidegger subordinates both *beyng* and *nonbeying* (construed in the current context as divine emptiness) to overarching metaphysical laws or principles of modality. Give their avowedly non-metaphysical stance, neither Heidegger nor the *Streit* theologian can consistently embrace any such position. At other times, Heidegger either collapses modality into the non-metaphysical event of *beyng*—a suggestion that proves to be untenable for several reasons, as we will see—or simply insists that all possibility and necessity somehow arise non-metaphysically from the "fissure" or tension between *beyng* and *Da-sein* without elaborating how. Once we have worked through the forgoing complexities, we will be better prepared to set forth a more plausible proposal in the following chapter.

Emptiness as Creative, Delineative, and Captivating

Elsewhere in his writings, Heidegger has more to say about a jug's inner recess. He reiterates its creative role: "The jug's void determines all the handling in the process of making the vessel."[5] However, the void's activity is not limited to the mere production of a vessel:

> The jug's jug character [which is inseparable from the jug's void] consists in the poured gift of the pouring out. . . . The giving of the outpouring can be a drink. The outpouring gives water, it gives wine to drink. The spring stays on in the water of the gift. In the spring the rock dwells, and in the rock dwells the dark slumber of the earth, which receives the rain and the dew of the sky. In the water of the spring dwells the marriage of sky and earth. . . . The gift of the pouring is a drink for mortals. It quenches their thirst. It refreshes their leisure. It enlivens their conviviality. But the jug's gift is at times also given for consecration.[6]

According to Heidegger's poetic encapsulation, "In the gift of this outpouring earth and sky, divinities and mortals dwell *together at once*."[7] These

5. Heidegger, "Thing," 169.
6. Heidegger, "Thing," 172.
7. Heidegger, "Thing," 173.

remarks attribute two additional activities to the essential emptiness that is the jug's void. To unpack them, it will be instructive to consider several related passages.

Meditating on a painting of a pair of empty peasant shoes by Van Gogh, Heidegger observes:

> From the dark opening of the worn insides of the shoes the toil-some tread of the worker stands forth. In the stiffly rugged heaviness of the shoes there is the accumulated tenacity of her slow trudge through the far-spreading and ever-uniform furrows of the field swept by a raw wind. On the leather lie the dampness and richness of the soil. Under the soles slides the loneliness of the field-path as evening falls. In the shoes vibrates the silent call of the earth, its quiet gift of the ripening grain and its unexpected self-refusal in fallow desolation of the wintry field.[8]

Through van Gogh's painting we experience the shoes' worn emptiness, which then expands our attention to include the peasant woman and various other beings that constitute an integral part of her daily rural existence. Thus besides enabling the shoes to exist in the first place, their worn emptiness also allows the entire world of the peasant woman to flare up in our awareness. The jug defined by its inner recess performs a similar delineative function by evoking the earth, sky, divinities, and mortals of the world in which it is used to pour water or wine that refreshes or consecrates.

Heidegger also describes how an ancient Greek temple *in situ* plays the same delineative role:

> A building, a Greek temple, portrays nothing. It simply stands there in the middle of the rock-cleft valley. The building encloses the figure of the god, and in this concealment lets it stand out into the holy precinct through the open portico. . . . The temple-work stands there, opens up a world and at the same time sets this world back again on earth, which itself only thus emerges as native ground. . . . The temple, in standing there, first gives to things their look and to men their outlook on themselves.[9]

Enclosing the holy space of its own inner sanctum, the temple acts paradoxically as a kind of opaque lens that brings the sheer granite walls of the valley into sharper focus for its ancient inhabitants as nurturing native soil.

8. Heidegger, "Origin of the Work of Art," 33–34.
9. Heidegger, "Origin of the Work of Art," 41–43.

Even today, many centuries later, the ruins of an empty temple may enable us to share dimly in an awareness of its bygone world.

A third activity performed by the jug's essential emptiness becomes apparent from how its gift of pouring a drink of water or a draft of wine can enliven conviviality or consecrate worship. The pouring draws human beings into fellowship with each other at a specific time and place. Similarly, the vacantness of a forest glade can bring people together at midnight around a celebratory bonfire or at noon during a ceremony in which they officially pledge themselves to preserving the surrounding forest tract. Recall from chapter 4 that Heidegger uses the term "captivation" for the spatial aspect of the time-space structuring what he calls the abyssal ground:

> This captivation is the *embrace* in which the moment and thus the temporalization are held fast (like the *originary* abyssal ground? "Emptiness"? Neither that nor fullness). This captivation also makes possible a bestowal as an essential possibility, grants bestowal a space.[10]

In light of Heidegger's willingness at least to consider emptiness in connection with captivation that bestows a space for essential possibilities—including communal ones like genuine conviviality, consecration, and commitment—we may appropriate this terminology to designate the captivating capacity of essential emptiness to facilitate various forms of human association in its immediate vicinity.

Occasionally, essential emptiness exercises all three roles of creating, delineating, and captivating simultaneously. Imagine the interior vault of an active church on a solemn day of worship. Not only does the interior vault create by allowing the church walls, windows, floor, and ceiling to gather around itself, it also captivates by beckoning the community of worshippers into the space it bestows, as well as delineates by sharpening their awareness of the sacred implements and acts that are indispensable to the worshippers' understanding of their place in the world as devout believers.

Notice that whether we are encountering the jug's void, the peasant shoes' worn emptiness, the glade's vacant expanse, or the church's interior vault, typically our experience is not fraught with the paralyzing anxiety of having to make some decision about God that we don't know how to make. Instead, the relevant experiences ranging from conviviality and camaraderie to pensive reflection, dignified dedication, reverent joy and transfixed

---

10. Heidegger, *Contributions to Philosophy*, 303.

ardor are all overwhelmingly positive, enriching, and life-affirming. In each case, we do not find ourselves stuck before some invisible crossroads; instead, we know exactly what to do when the cup is extended to us, when others quietly join us in front of the painting, when the bonfire is lit, the oath is administered, or the worship service begins. Equating the divinity of the last god with essential emptiness would therefore make it possible to transfer the definite phenomenology and clear praxis associated with the latter to the former.

Admittedly, there are times when human beings encounter anxiety or indecision in the vicinity of essentially empty divinity. Heidegger himself alludes to "uncomplaining anxiety as to the certainty of bread" and "shivering at the surrounding menace of death"[11] that pervades the worn emptiness of the peasant shoes painted by van Gogh. The wine might be poured from the jug to ease the grief of a family mourning the seemingly senseless loss of a child, the glade may summon witnesses who are stunned by the environmental damage that has already been inflicted on the forest tract, the church could shelter members who are struggling with hurt feelings and uncertainty over the future of their congregation. Yet in many other places and times, the vicinity of essential nothingness is suffused with overwhelmingly affirmative feelings coupled with calm determination. If God is essential emptiness, then we have no proof but at least some hope that the positive purposefulness we enjoy so often in its vicinity will eventually hold sway wherever and whenever it creates, delineates, or captivates.

A lingering question is why the jug's inner recess, the peasant shoe's worn emptiness, the vacant glade, the temple's holy sanctum, and the church's interior vault are all manifestations of one and the same essential nothingness as opposed to distinct voids in their own right. From a religious perspective, the answer must be that viewing each creating, delineating, or captivating hollowness as unitary nothingness is a choice of faith rather than a dictate of reason. The DEN proposal is the audacious idea of God as a single creative, delineative, and captivating vacuum at work in the vicinity of any nullity where one or more of these functions is being performed. Heidegger's suggestion in the *Beiträge* that the *hohle Mitte* of any particular jug is an open realm in which beings come to stand already anticipates this idea. For a Christian, the important question is whether it is theologically pregnant. There is already some reason to think so, since the phenomenological and practical dimensions the DEN proposal attributes

11. Heidegger, "Origin of the Work of Art," 34.

to divine essential nothingness promise to circumvent the Heideggerian theological dilemma, and since divine essential nothingness's trifold activity allows room for Trinitarian speculation.

Of course, much more would need to be explained, including how divine essential nothingness not only creates a jug from the sides and base or a church from the walls, windows, floor, and ceiling but also creates the sides, base, walls, windows, floor, and ceiling themselves.[12] Heidegger himself says nothing further about the matter, which is unsurprising in light of his indifference toward the issue of divine creation and other theological questions. Nevertheless, the *Streit* theologian might find it well worth the effort to try to develop her own comprehensive explanation of divine essential nothingness's creative activity—as long as the DEN proposal does not suffer from a more serious flaw.

An Unresolved Ambiguity: Modality and das Nichts

The proponent of the DEN proposal conceives of God as essentially a creating, delineating, and captivating nothingness that encompasses both total ontological negation in which there are no human or non-human beings whatsoever and the sheltering of the non-metaphysical event in the totality of beings through the grounding activity of fully emergent *Da-sein* as distinct *possibilities*. Hence it is natural to wonder exactly what relation obtains between divine nothingness and the modal properties of possibility and necessity. In order to remain true to the Heideggerian roots of the DEN proposal, let us consider some of what Heidegger says about modality in the *Beiträge*, where he discusses it primarily in connection with *beyng*. His remarks on the topic vacillate between two poles.

---

12. At some point, does the creative activity of divine essential nothingness "bottom out" in pre-existing elements coming together around its open realm to form the first complex created entities, which then come together to form more complex entities, and so forth? Such a view is incompatible with Christian orthodoxy's doctrine of creation *ex nihilo*, according to which God creates everything other than Himself from nothing. Or instead is the universe infinitely divisible into things made out of atoms, atoms made out of subatomic particles, the latter made out of even tinier particles, and so on *ad infinitum*, in which case whatever entities exist *ad extra* do so through the coming together of less complex entities around the open realm of divine essential nothingness? Arguably, the latter view can accommodate creation *ex nihilo*.

Sometimes Heidegger seems to subordinate the non-metaphysical event of appropriation or *beyng* to modal categories. A paradigmatic instance is the following passage:

> Thinking, as inceptual, grounds the time-space in its structure of transporting and captivating and penetrates the fissure of beyng in the uniqueness, freedom, contingency, necessity, possibility, and actuality of the essential occurrence of beyng.[13]

Here, overarching modal principles of contingency, necessity, possibility, and actuality appear to govern the essential occurrence of the non-metaphysical event by penetrating its so-called "fissure." Certainly the essential (i.e., non-distorted) occurrence of the event in "the other beginning" is possible; otherwise, Heidegger would not be trying to prepare for it. For the same reason the event's essential occurrence is not necessary, since then it would eventually have to happen no matter what Heidegger or anyone else does. If someday the non-metaphysical event of *beyng* does essentially occur, then it will become an actuality that remains contingent since it might never have occurred.[14]

At one point Heidegger explicitly elevates possibility over the essential occurrence of *beyng*, which includes the last god's mysterious indigence, by making the former the origin of the latter:

> The *beyng* of such essential occurrence is itself unique in this essence. For it essentially occurs as the stroke which has perhaps already announced itself as the extreme possibility of the decision of Western history, the possibility that *beyng* itself, of such an essence, arises as the indigence of the god, who needs the stewardship of the human being. This possibility is itself the origin "of" *beyng*, and what, according to the previous opinion about *beyng*, seems substantiated here in speaking of the most general and the

---

13. Heidegger, *Contributions to Philosophy*, 187.

14. Other commentators have picked up on Heidegger's tendency to subordinate the non-metaphysical event of appropriation or *Ereignis* to modal contingency. Polt claims that *Da-sein*'s becoming at home in the event of appropriation "is not an escape from beings, but an opportunity to dwell among them in a way that appreciates appropriation as a contingent event, and thus freely and authentically to inhabit what is one's own" (Polt, *Emergency of Being*, 142). See also Pöggeler, "'Historicity' in Heidegger's Late Work," 63, translation modified in Polt, *Emergency of Being*, 142n3: "Every pure work of art . . . lets the history of Truth be seen as that which possibly might not have been, i.e., as event (*Ereignis*)."

trans-historical is entirely, above all, the purely and simply, the unique and the historical.[15]

Heidegger suggests that in addition to falling under the modal categories of possibility and contingency, *beyng* is also governed by a kind of necessity. For example, he hints that the metaphysical misunderstanding culminating in our contemporary plight *must* first take place if *beyng* is someday to occur essentially: "The necessity of the *plight*. Plight of what? Of *beyng* itself, which must bring into the open, and thus overcome, its first beginning through the other beginning."[16]

Even if the aforementioned plight is contingent rather than necessary, another kind of necessity is said to inhere in the very nature of *beyng*:

> *The essence of truth is untruth.* This statement, deliberately formulated to be in conflict with itself, is supposed to express the fact that the *negative* belongs intrinsically to truth, by no means as a sheer lack but as resistance, as that self-concealing which comes into the clearing as such. Thereby the original relation of truth to *beyng* as event is grasped.[17]

As an event of truth whereby beings become disclosed to us, *beyng*" itself— even in its essential, non-distorted, non-metaphysical occurrence—*cannot* become completely disclosed to us but *must* always to some extent remain self-concealed.[18]

Elsewhere in the *Beiträge*, however, Heidegger presents a very different picture of the relation between *beyng* and the modalities:

> The "modalities" pertain to beings (to beingness) and say nothing at all about the fissure of *beyng* itself. This fissure can come into question only if the truth of *beyng* as event lights up, specifically as that of which the god has need in such a way that the human being belongs intrinsically to the event. . . . The modalities thereby

---

15. Heidegger, *Contributions to Philosophy*, 381–82.

16. Heidegger, *Contributions to Philosophy*, 260. Polt writes: "However, Heidegger often implies that be-ing *has* to withdraw. This suggests an insight into a necessity, which calls for an elucidation" (Polt, *Emergency of Being*, 142). The hyphenated "be-ing" is Polt's preferred English translation for Heidegger's original *Seyn*.

17. Heidegger, *Contributions to Philosophy*, 281.

18. "This means that the inception, be-ing itself, cannot be grounded—it is an 'abyss' that can never be articulated conclusively" (Polt, *Emergency of Being*, 145).

fall short of the fissure, just as beingness falls short of the truth of *beyng*.[19]

On this conception, there are no metaphysically prior principles of possibility and necessity that apply not only to beings but also to *beyng* itself. Instead, genuine possibility and necessity only emerge within the "fissure" between *beyng* and humans working toward becoming full-blown *Da-sein* by clearing way enough confusion for the last god to pass by them rather than abscond.

With regard to possibility, only if *beyng* occurs does it become possible to misunderstand it metaphysically as a maximally general characteristic or to understand it properly as a non-metaphysical event of appropriation:

> The *possible* essentially occurs in *beyng* alone and as its deepest fissure, so that in the thinking of the other beginning *beyng* must first be thought in form of the possible. . . . What is possible, and indeed the possible as such, opens itself only to an attempt.[20]

The same is true of necessity: "Out of this plight the grounding of the truth of being, the grounding of *Da-sein*, becomes necessary"[21]; "Yet necessities shone forth only in a plight."[22] Heidegger seems to have in mind the conditional necessity of a particular possibility that only emerges within the happening of *beyng*: namely, if we are in a plight where *beyng* has withdrawn due to metaphysical confusion, then necessarily the plight can only be overcome by our clearing away such confusion.[23]

No one seeking to develop a *Streit* theology rooted in Christian faith should be receptive to the second conception of modality found in the *Beiträge*. The reason is plain. If all necessity, contingency, actuality, and

---

19. Heidegger, *Contributions to Philosophy*, 219–21.

20. Heidegger, *Contributions to Philosophy*, 374.

21. Heidegger, *Contributions to Philosophy*, 24.

22. Heidegger, *Contributions to Philosophy*, 77.

23. Polt contrasts what he calls "relatively contingent" and "relatively necessary" modes of *beyng*'s self-concealment: relative to the event of *beyng*, the metaphysical "oblivion of being" is contingent since "this seems to be a happening that could have been otherwise," whereas relative to the metaphysical distinction between beings and being the oblivion itself is necessary since "in order to grasp the *idea*, or the beingness of beings, the Greeks had to remain oblivious to be-ing" (Polt, *Emergency of Being*, 143). That is, failing to grasp the essentially non-metaphysical nature of *beyng* as event is necessary in order to postulate being as the maximally general characteristic shared by beings. Polt's contrast fits well with the second Heideggerian conception of modality as emerging only within the "fissure" between *beyng* and humans.

possibility are grounded in the "fissure" between *beyng* and humans, then the very possibility of a last god—including the possibilities of its either appearing to us or remaining hidden from us—depends on human participation in the event. Yet Christian orthodoxy is committed to the doctrine that divinity *per se* is entirely independent from all human and non-human beings, the event of *beyng*, or anything else *ad extra*. God would still be God even in the condition of total ontological negation where there was and never has been anything else.[24] Furthermore, this condition of total ontological negation is contingent, in that although there is nothing other than God it is still *possible* for God to create something other than Himself. To be sure, it is only possible for divinity to appear or not to appear to humans if there are human beings. But the possibility of human beings to whom divinity can either appear or not appear is already anticipated in the condition of total ontological negation where there is nothing and never has been anything else besides divinity. Consequently, at least some modal facts are, like divinity itself, independent of any human participation in *beyng*.

One might reply, "So much the worse for the misguided project of developing a Christian *Streit* theology." Unlike the God of Christianity, the last god intimated in the *Beiträge* cannot be separated from the possibility of its appearing or not appearing to us, which in turn essentially depends on our participation in the event of *beyng*. Heidegger basically implies as much with his insistence that the indigence of the god *needs* the stewardship of the human being who belongs intrinsically to the event. Despite some ambiguity on Heidegger's part, the true "collision of necessity and possibility," including the necessity of removing metaphysical confusion so that it becomes possible for the last god to pass us by, only unfolds within the "fissure" between *beyng* and humans. The notion of any modal facts obtaining independently of our participation in the event is just another metaphysical misstep, "what truly belongs to that which 'ontology' treats as the pale and vacuous *jumble* of modalities."[25]

The foregoing reply, and more generally with the picture of modality lying behind it, can be buttressed with from an argument sketched by Richard Polt:

24. Interestingly, sometimes Heidegger seems to acknowledge divine independence: "'The gods' do not need *beyng* as their proper domain, in which they themselves find a place to stand," though he immediately goes on to add that the gods "require beyng so that through *beyng*, which does not belong to them, they might indeed belong to themselves" (Heidegger, *Contributions to Philosophy*, 346).

25. Heidegger, *Contributions to Philosophy*, 222.

With the "fissure," the *Contributions* go farther than *Being and Time*: they indicate a plurality within the happening of be-ing itself, which is irreducible to presence. The traditional doctrine of modalities will be insufficient here, because it speaks only of necessity, actuality, and possibility as aspects of presence as the being of beings. We need a way of finding plurality within the *giving* of the being of beings. The doctrine of modalities can provide some inspiration for this project, but we must resist the temptation to draw up an ahistorical table of modalities in the traditional manner.[26]

By construing modal properties merely as aspects of present beings, the argument runs, the traditional doctrine is insufficient because it precludes any explanation of how all necessity, actuality, and possibility arise from the event of *beyng* itself. Nonetheless, since the traditional doctrine is correct in withholding modal properties from nonbeing, it makes some contribution to the project of grounding all modality in *beyng*.

The trouble with Polt's argument is that it is not at all evident why it is correct to withhold modal properties from nonbeing. Consider again a condition of total ontological negation devoid of any universe and thus of any time-space, any event of *beyng* (whether confusedly or clearly understood), and any human or non-human beings whatsoever. Presumably, such was the situation "before" the Big Bang. This kind of nonbeing is not necessary but contingent, since even if it obtains, the possibility (which, indeed, eventually becomes an actuality) for there to be such a universe remains. It is not like the "negative fact" consisting of there being nothing that is both a perfect square and a perfect circle. The latter kind of nonbeing is necessary rather than contingent, since for there to be something that is both perfectly square and perfectly circular is impossible. If the envisioned condition of total ontological negation is contingent in the absence of the "fissure" between *beyng* and humans, then contrary to Polt's argument in support of the second conception of modality in the *Beiträge*, at least some modal facts *are* independent of human participation in the event. It may even be true that divinity, like these modal facts, is also radically independent from *beyng*, *Da-sein*, time-space, or anything else *ad extra*.[27]

At the end of the *Beiträge*, Heidegger returns to the ambiguity concerning the interrelations among divinity, *beyng*, and modality:

26. Polt, *Emergency of Being*, 151.

27. For further discussion of the relation between nonbeing and modality see Dillard, *Heidegger and Philosophical Atheology*, 89–99; *Way into Scholasticism*, 117–19.

> In what does the divinity of the gods consist? Why *beyng*? Because
> of the gods? Why gods? Because of *beyng*? *The appropriating event*
> and the possibility of the *why!* Can the "why" still be made a tribu-
> nal before which *beyng* is to be haled? But why the *truth* of *beyng*?
> This truth belongs to the essence of *beyng!*[28]

He then makes a last-ditch effort to resolve the ambiguity: "Why *beyng*? Out
of itself. But what is itself? The creative grounding of *beyng*, of its ground,
is the 'between' of *beyng* as abyssal ground."[29] His suggestion seems to be
that "out of itself," *beyng* grounds not only the various possibilities and necessities pertaining to beings but also its own possibility. This flat-footed
declaration is patently unsatisfactory in the absence of a plausible account
of how the possibility of *beyng* emerges even in a contingent condition of
total ontological negation that is entirely devoid of *beyng*. No such account
is to be found anywhere in the *Beiträge*.

Heidegger's failure to explain how all modality is grounded in the
"fissure" between humans and the event of *beyng* is fatal for the initially
attractive DEN proposal. Creating, delineating, and captivating divine
nothingness supposedly enfolds contingent total ontological negation,
beyng metaphysically distorted by humans who have not attained *Da-sein*,
and *beyng* non-metaphysically sheltered in beings by humans who have attained *Da-sein* as different possible ontological conditions. If the possibility
of these respective conditions is not grounded in the "fissure," then apparently there are overarching metaphysical laws or principles of modality that
govern divine nonbeing, non-divine nonbeing, *beyng*, and all human or
non-human beings after all. Therefore, a Christian *Streit* theology that (1) is
avowedly non-metaphysical, (2) draws upon the philosophy of Heidegger's
Beiträge, and (3) appeals to the DEN proposal in order to overcome the
theological predicament in which the latter work leaves us is an unstable
mishmash of metaphysical and non-metaphysical thinking.

Fortunately, there is one more theological proposal to evaluate. The
next chapter will, among other things, consider how the third proposal
traces all modality back to divinity itself without resorting to any metaphysical apparatus.

---

28. Heidegger, *Contributions to Philosophy*, 400.
29. Heidegger, *Contributions to Philosophy*, 400.

Chapter 8

A Heidegerrian Theology of the Cross

Christ is the Answer (sign outside Tucson, Arizona)

THE SPLENDOR OF THE SIMPLE

IN 1947, HEIDEGGER COMPOSED a short work entitled "The Thinker as Poet" (*Aus der Erfahrung des Denkens*). Alternating simple poetic lines that depict the rustic environs of Heidegger's Todtnauberg cabin encountered at various hours of the day and seasons of the year with prolix philosophical commentary concerning being, man, the gods, and the dangers of muddled philosophizing, the text attempts to display the respective ways in which poetry and thinking each seek to articulate a radically non-metaphysical understanding of the world.

Like the poem from Pattiann Rogers quoted at the beginning of chapter 6, Heidegger's Todtnauberg verses evoke a strong sense of the rural world's ephemerality, coupled with an excited expectation of standing on the brink of some extraordinary revelation. For example,

> When the early morning light quietly grows above the mountains
> . . .

> When the little windwheel outside the cabin window sings in the gathering thunderstorm . . .

> When through a rent in the rain-clouded sky a ray of the sun sud-
> denly glides over the gloom of the meadows . . .

> When in early summer lonely narcissi bloom hidden in the mead-
> ow and the rock-rose gleams under the maple . . .[1]

Suddenly, in his philosophical gloss immediately following the lonely nar-
cissi verse, Heidegger introduces a surprising new phrase: "The splendor of
the simple."[2] What does he mean by that?

Late in the *Beiträge*, Heidegger briefly addresses the notion of simplicity (*Einfachheit*), which he regards as an aspect of the essential, non-
distorted, and non-metaphysical occurrence of *beyng*:

> But the gods and humans do not first assume their respective in-
> digence and stewardship as a property; it is rather the case that
> they draw their essence from these. *Beyng* is the need of the gods
> and, as needing *Da-sein*, is more abyssal than anything which may
> be called a being and which can no longer be named by *beyng*.
> . . . Without mediation, the "between" essentially occurs as the
> ground of the ones en-countering each other in this ground. That
> determines the simplicity of the "between," a simplicity which is
> not emptiness, but is instead the ground of the fullness arising out
> of the en-counter as strife.[3]

Heidegger seems to have the following in mind. The encounter between
the gods and *Da-sein* is a complex phenomenon, since it consists in distinct
"relata"—i.e., the gods and *Da-sein*—coming together through strife into a
unity. This complex coming together is mediated by *beyng*, which the gods
need in order so that human misconceptions distorting divinity are cleared
away, and which in turn needs *Da-sein* as the site where the clearing work
of *beyng* can unfold. Yet *beyng* itself is not a complex phenomenon, since it
does not consist in two or more distinct "relata" coming together into unity
through the mediation of something else. Thus relative to the encounter
of strife between the gods and *Da-sein*, *beyng* in its essential occurrence is
simple.[4]

---

1. Heidegger, "Thinker as Poet," 4–7.

2. Heidegger, "Thinker as Poet," 7.

3. Heidegger, *Contributions to Philosophy*, 370–71.

4. As Vallega-Neu observes, "The 'simpleness' of en-owning [*beyng*] is determined
by the in-between (*Zwischen*) that occurs without mediation as 'the ground of the coun-
tering ones in it'" (Vallega-Neu, *Heidegger's "Contributions to Philosophy,"* 113).

But such an abstract characterization of the simplicity of *beyng* as the "between" of the gods and *Da-sein* does not even begin to explain how *beyng* in its non-mediated simplicity fosters a powerful encounter between human beings who are on their way to attaining full *Da-sein* and divinity in the guise of the last god. Phenomenologically, the vertiginous trembling and dizzying oscillation *Da-sein* experiences in grounding the non-metaphysical event of appropriation is merely another manifestation of anxiety in the face of something uncanny. In the present instance, the uncanny something is the non-metaphysical event of appropriation itself, or *beyng*. Theologically, this anxiety arises from emerging *Da-sein's* finding itself in the predicament of having to make a fateful decision about the last god that neither *beyng* nor anything else at the disposal of emerging *Da-sein* enables it to make.

One might conclude that Heidegger's notion of simplicity is simply too vague to be of any use and hence should be discarded. However, there is an alternative response. Perhaps the problem is not so much with Heidegger's notion of simplicity itself but with Heidegger's claim that simplicity is fundamentally an aspect of *beyng*. Instead, as a kind of theological experiment, suppose that we apply the Heideggerian terms "the splendor of the simple" and "simplicity" to the last god or divinity. In order to evaluate the outcome of the experiment, we must answer three questions. First, does identifying divinity with Heideggerian simplicity enable us to overcome the theological predicament of having to decide about the last god without knowing how to decide? Second, does the identification in question confront any formidable conceptual obstacles? Third, if such obstacles do arise, then does anything in Heidegger's later philosophy suggest how they can be surmounted? The present chapter will argue for an affirmative answer to all three questions. What eventually materializes is a decidedly Christological proposal that is clearly superior both to the previous two proposals and that can serve as the cornerstone for the sought-for theology of *Streit* rooted in the Christian faith.

A Cul-de-Sac, an Escape Hatch, and a New Challenge

Let us begin by reminding ourselves of how Heidegger describes the relation between the passing by of the last god and the essential occurrence of *beyng* sufficiently free of metaphysical distortions:

> The trembling of the coming to be of the oscillation in the turning, the appropriation of the belonging, grounding, sheltering *Da-sein* to the intimation—this essential occurrence of *beyng* is not itself the last god; instead, the essential occurrence of being [*beyng*] grounds the sheltering, and thereby the creative preservation, of the god, who *pervades beyng with divinity* always only in work and sacrifice, deed and thought.[5]

Once the last god's need for *beyng* has been fulfilled through the clearing away of human misconceptions about divinity, the last god reciprocally pervades *beyng* with its own clarified divinity. Since the last god is said to pervade *beying* with divinity through the works and deeds of human beings who "shelter" *beyng* in tools, artworks, and other non-human beings amidst a purely contingent totality of beings that might never have been and might someday no longer be, the last god can also be said to pervade not just *beyng* but also the remaining ontological conditions of emerging *Da-sein*, particular non-human beings, the totality of beings, and total non-being with its own divinity.[6]

Next, let us recognize that if the last god in its own divinity is splendidly simple, then it cannot be a unity consisting of distinct "relata." An immediate consequence is that whenever the last god pervades one or more ontological conditions with its own divinity, its divinity is wholly available within each of them. It is not as if different pieces or separate parts of the last god are scattered among emerging *Da-sein*, each particular non-human being, the totality of beings, the non-metaphysical event of *beyng* in its essential occurrence, and total nonbeing. Rather, whenever we are confronted with any one of these ontological conditions we are already encountering the last god's splendidly simple divinity in its entirety.[7]

---

5. Heidegger, *Contributions to Philosophy*, 206.

6. Although he is working within a philosophical context quite different from Heidegger's, Pseudo-Dionysius also stresses how the ubiquity of divinity pervades every stratum of created reality: "He [God] is called perfect, both as without increase, and as always perfect, and as undiminished, as pre-holding all things in Himself, and overflowing as beseems one, inexhaustible, and same, and super-full, and undiminished, abundance, in accordance with which He perfects all perfect things, and fills them with His own perfection" (Pseudo-Dionysius, "On Divine Names," 122).

7. Elsewhere, Pseudo-Dionysius gives another instructive example of how divinity is not excluded from even the lowliest level of creation: "I will also add, that which seems to be more dishonorable than all, and the most incongruous, viz. that distinguished theologians have shown it [supreme divinity] to us as representing Itself under the form of a worm" (Pseudo-Dionysius, "On the Heavenly Hierarchy," 12).

Finally, let us recall the theological predicament in which we found ourselves at the end of Heidegger's *Beiträge*. The uncanny divinity of the last god transcends not only our own emerging *Da-sein* but also any particular non-human being, the contingent totality of beings, the non-distorted event of *beyng*, and the possibility of total nonbeing. Nevertheless, we are required to reach a fateful decision that will result either in the last god's powerfully passing us by or remaining forever hidden from us—even though we have nothing to go on in reaching this decision except the foregoing ontological conditions, no one of which is the last god itself. As a consequence, we are wracked with anxiety. Yet in a striking religious reversal, the splendor of simple divinity appears to offer an escape hatch out of this theological cul-de-sac. For, since the last god fully pervades every ontological condition in the "other beginning" Heidegger envisions, by confronting any one of them we are already encountering the last god itself. Accordingly, our anxiety in the face of uncanny divinity gives way to our trembling excitement before the last god to be found right at our fingertips.

Yet now a new challenge looms on the horizon, one that threatens to upset the entire applecart. If the last god fully pervades *Da-sein*, any particular non-human being, the totality of beings, the non-metaphysical event of *beyng*, and total nonbeing, then it appears to follow that each of these five ontological conditions is fully divine. Furthermore, if the last god in its divinity is splendidly simple, then all of the ontological conditions fully sharing in its divinity are also splendidly simple. We then seem committed to the highly counterintuitive consequence that *Da-sein*, any particular non-human being, the totality of beings, etc. are not really distinct from one another but instead are all one and the same. Otherwise, the divinity of the last god fully pervading them would be divided against itself in a plurality of distinct ontological conditions and hence not be splendidly simple.[8] Any such monolithic monism is problematic both philosophi-

8. A possible precedent of the same challenge arises for Nicholas of Cusa's discussion of divine uniqueness, equality, and union. According to Nicholas, God is a unique individual. Divinity also stands in the relation of being equally unique to any other unique individual as well as to itself, so that divine uniqueness is reflexively united with itself through this same relation. The crucial question is whether divine uniqueness, equality, and union are the same as the uniqueness, equality, and union of created beings. Given Nicholas's commitment to divine infinity as limitlessness, the answer seems to be yes; otherwise, divinity would be excluded from created beings and thus God would be limited in some way. Yet Nicholas also takes divinity to be absolutely simple, so that there is no real plurality within divine uniqueness, equality, and union. But then there is no real plurality within the uniqueness, equality, and union of created "things" either. See especially Nicholas of Cusa, "On Learned Ignorance," 14–16.

cally and theologically: philosophically, because it demands that we reject our commonsense experience of real ontological plurality in the world as purely illusory[9]; theologically, because it implies a coalescing of divinity and the world that is incompatible with the Christian insistence on God's transcendence and total independence from creation.

To avoid the unwelcome consequence of monolithic monism, we might try to block the inference from the premise that the last god fully pervades a given ontological condition to the conclusion that the last god and the ontological condition are one and the same. Unfortunately, Heidegger does not explain the notion of *fully pervading*. In the absence of any further elaboration, we are left unable to draw a principled distinction between the case in which X fully pervades Y and the case in which X and Y are one and the same. Heidegger is equally mum about the notion of splendid simplicity, making it impossible for us to argue that something might be splendidly simple throughout a plurality of really distinct ontological conditions.

Still, Heidegger's brief foray into combining poetry with thinking features another curious turn of phrase: "Pain gives of its healing power where we least expect it."[10] Fortunately, Heidegger does say more about *pain*. Let us turn our attention to how some of what he says might be used to overcome the new challenge of monolithic monism.

Trakl's Pain and Divine Distinctness

In his philosophical commentary on the poetry of Georg Trakl, Heidegger declares: "The nature of pain is in itself the converse."[11] His gloss on the third stanza of Trakl's poem "A Winter Evening" begins to elucidate what he has in mind. The stanza runs:

> Wanderer quietly steps within;
> Pain has turned the threshold to stone.
> There lie, in limpid brightness shown,
> Upon the table bread and wine.[12]

9. The idea that plurality is an illusion is reminiscent of the absolute idealism defended in Bradley, *Appearance and Reality*.

10. Heidegger, "Thinker as Poet," 7.

11. Heidegger, "Language in the Poem," 185.

12. Trakl quoted in Heidegger, "Language," 210. For the original German text version of the poem, see Trakl, *Die Dichtungen*, 126.

Heidegger comments, "The third stanza calls world and things into the middle of their intimacy. The seam that binds their being toward one another is pain."[13] On Heidegger's reading, pain for Trakl is not primarily an unpleasant sensation but rather a transitional zone (e.g., the threshold of a dwelling) in which different things (e.g., a wanderer, a table set with bread and wine) come together into worldly unity through activities occurring within the zone (e.g., the wanderer's stepping over the threshold into the dwelling where the table is set). Since these activities are often marked by what Trakl calls "darksome courses"[14] of struggle and hardship, "pain" is an apt poetic term for the transitional zone in which they unfold. In addition to "the converse," Heidegger employs more philosophical terms like "the gentle two-fold"[15] and "apartness"[16] to describe the same zone.

Interestingly for our purposes, Heidegger also detects a connection in Trakl's poetry between divinity and pain as the transitional zone fraught with negative affectivity. Trakl uses the color blue to evoke the holy: "And in holy blueness shining footfalls rung forth . . . the holiness of blue flowers . . . moves the beholder . . . Animal face/Freezes with blueness, with its holiness."[17] Heidegger remarks: "The language that this poetry speaks stems from this transition [in pain]. Its path leads from the downfall of all that decays over to the descent into the twilit blue of the holy."[18]

The Eucharistic overtones of bread and wine lying in limpid brightness on the table in "A Winter Evening" and the allusion to transfiguration in another poem[19] obviously have a decidedly Christian resonance. Even so, Heidegger is quick to reject any Christian interpretation of Trakl:

> If indeed this poet is so resolute a Christian, why does he not, here in the extreme agony of his last saying [in Trakl's late poem "Lament"] call out to God and Christ? Why does he instead name "the sister's swaying shadow" and call her "the greeting one"? Why does the song end with the name of the "unborn grandsons" and

13. Heidegger, "Language," 205.

14. For the occurrence of this phrase in Trakl's poem, see Trakl, *Die Dichtungen*, 194. For Heidegger's commentary on the phrase see Heidegger, "Language," 200.

15. See Heidegger, "Language in the Poem," 174.

16. See Heidegger, "Langauge in the Poem," 172.

17. For these verses and corresponding references, see Heidegger, "Language in the Poem," 166.

18. Heidegger, "Language in the Poem," 191.

19. See, for example, "Verklärung" ["Transfiguration"] (Trakl, *Die Dicthungen*, 144). Heidegger briefly discusses this poem in Heidegger, "Language in the Poem," 183–84.

> not with the confident hope of Christian redemption? Why does
> the sister also appear in the other late poem, "Lament"? Why is
> eternity called there "the icy wave"? Is this Christian thinking? It is
> not even Christian despair.[20]

Heidegger's terse rejection assumes that naming the sister and her swaying
shadow, the unborn grandsons, and the icy wave is not a way of calling out
to God and Christ. However, if splendidly simple divinity fully pervades
every ontological condition, then the twilit blue of the holy is immediately
available to us in each of these human and non-human beings. Their names
may then double as divine names we can use to call out to God. And once
God is in the picture, the possibility of a thoroughly Christian understanding of His "holy blueness" cannot be ruled out *a priori*. It remains for us to
elaborate this Christian understanding in order to overcome the threat of
monolithic monism.

THE PHENOMENOLOGICAL DYNAMICS
OF THE CRUCIFIXION

In chapter 2, we observed how the contrariety principle at the heart of
Luther's *theologia crucis* functions as a kind of key or legend that enables
us to decrypt the paradoxical presence of divine power and wisdom hidden under their contrary forms of human weakness, folly, and suffering
throughout a range of negatively affective situations. The nerve of the following theological proposal is similar: phenomenological reflection on the
circumstances of Christ's crucifixion functions as a key to deciphering the
appearance of the last god's heretofore elusive divinity, yielding what may
be called a Heideggerian theology of the cross.

Where is God during Jesus's crucifixion? To make the question a bit
more vivid, to what would a Christian person of faith point if she were
asked to indicate where God is encountered in this perceptible episode? In
light of her faith that Jesus of Nazareth is also divine, obviously she would
point to the human being who is suffering and dying on the cross. Yet even
within the circumstances of the crucifixion, divinity is not restricted to the
man nailed to that instrument of torture and execution but can be found
in two additional places. One place is indicated by Jesus's crying out in a
loud voice, "My God, my God, why have you forsaken me?" (Matt 27:46;

---

20. Heidegger, "Language in the Poem," 193.

Mark 15:34). Here, divinity is addressed as standing in direct opposition to the cross, so that the Christian would not only point to the crucified Jesus but also into the middle distance before and above his heavenward-raised eyes. Another place where divinity can found is indicated by Jesus's assurance to the penitent criminal crucified beside him that "Amen, I say to you, today you will be with me in Paradise" (Luke 23:43) and, more generally, Jesus's promise of his impending resurrection from the dead. Thus in addition to the crucified Christ and the opposing middle distance before and above him, the Christian would gesture beyond the site of Jesus's execution toward where Jesus rises from the dead to walk on earth again with his disciples and to dwell with his friends in Paradise.

What the phenomenological dynamics of the crucifixion disclose to us, then, is a double converse in the appearance of divinity under those particular perceptible circumstances. Divinity fully pervades the man dying on the cross; but divinity in the middle distance is conversely opposite to the crucifixion, and post-resurrection divinity is conversely beyond the entire site and period of Jesus's execution. If we now read this double converse as the key to mapping the phenomenology of divinity whenever it appears, then divinity is always experientially encountered as conversely opposite to and conversely beyond any circumstances it fully pervades. *A fortiori*, the appearance of the splendidly simple last god is doubly converse to the five ontological conditions, each of which it also fully pervades provided that the condition obtains. To drive the point home, it will be useful to work through a couple of examples.

Consider the ontological condition of total nonbeing with no human or non-human beings and no occurrence of *beyng*. Although total nonbeing is devoid of any human beings to whom divinity might appear, we can certainly conceive of total nonbeing and ask how it relates to divinity. Since divinity fully pervades whatever ontological condition obtains, if total nonbeing obtains then divinity fully pervades it.[21] In fact, though, what

---

21. More can now be said about how divinity fully pervades an obtaining ontological condition. To anticipate a point made in the following section, boundlessness is traditionally associated with divinity. Boundlessness included in something is thus an indication of divinity in it; e.g., my boundless love for someone else is an indication of divinity abiding in me. On a more mundane level, boundlessness is included in any ontological condition, since if the latter obtains then boundlessly many other ontological conditions do not obtain; e.g., if total nonbeing obtains, then a universe with only one being in it does not obtain, a universe with only two beings in it does not obtains, etc. Divinity fully pervades any obtaining ontological condition through the latter condition's boundless exclusion of other ontological conditions.

currently obtains is not total nonbeing but a totality of beings, some human and some non-human. When this positive condition obtains, total nonbeing does not obtain. Since divinity fully pervades this positive ontological condition while total nonbeing does not obtain, divinity is not the same as total nonbeing. Divinity is therefore conversely beyond total nonbeing, since if total nonbeing does not obtain then divinity fully pervades whatever positive ontological condition obtains instead. Divinity is also conversely opposite to total nonbeing. For even if total nonbeing obtains, it and the divinity that fully pervades it are not the same.

Or consider an ontological condition in which *beyng* essentially occurs and hence is non-metaphysically sheltered by *Da-sein* in beings. If this ontological condition obtains, then divinity fully pervades it.[22] Yet if a condition in which *beyng* does not occur at all (e.g., total nonbeing or a condition where there are only nonhuman beings) or in which it only occurs inessentially (i.e., when humans misconstrue the event of *beyng* as a maximally general characteristic common to all beings) obtains, then this alternative condition is fully pervaded by divinity. Thus divinity is both conversely beyond *beyng*'s essential occurrence, since divinity fully pervades whatever ontological condition obtains instead of *beyng*'s essential occurrence, as well as conversely opposite to *beyng*'s essential occurrence, since even if *beyng* essentially occurs and so is fully pervaded by divinity, divinity remains distinct from the essential occurrence of *beyng*. A parallel argument can be constructed to show that divinity is both conversely beyond and conversely opposite to each of the other ontological conditions Heidegger recognizes.

It might be objected that divinity is not distinct from each ontological condition, but rather that any ontological condition is not only fully pervaded by but also the same as divinity so long as the condition in question obtains. Thus if total nothingness obtains, then divinity fully pervades and hence is the same as total nothingness so long as total nothingness obtains; if *beyng* essentially occurs, then divinity fully pervades and hence is the same as *beyng* so long as *beyng* essentially occurs, and so forth. In our current plight more than one ontological condition obtains, including myriad non-human beings, human beings who may potentially attain *Da-sein*,

---

22. Again, divinity fully pervades an essential occurrence of *beyng*, since if this latter ontological condition obtains then boundlessly many other ontological conditions do not: total nonbeing, an inessential occurrence of *beyng* with only 100 (101, 102, . . .) humans in it, another essential occurrence of *beyng* in which 1 (2, 3, . . .) more humans attain full-blown *Da-sein* than they do in the actual essential occurrence of *beyng*, etc.

a totality of beings, and an inessential occurrence of *beyng*. An immediate consequence is that divinity fully pervades and hence is the same as each non-human being, the totality of beings, and inessentially occurring *beyng*. Interestingly, Heidegger's tendency at times to speak of *gods* in the plural suggests how one might embrace this consequence while avoiding monolithic monism: in our current plight (or in a future scenario featuring non-human beings, *Da-sein*, a totality of beings and essentially occurring *beyng*), there is a multiplicity of splendidly simple last gods, one for each distinct and currently obtaining divinized ontological condition. In other words, a possible solution to monolithic monism is a kind of polytheism.[23]

Against any version of polytheism stands Heidegger's own insistence that "*Da-sein* does not count gods."[24] A passage from Part VII of the *Beiträge* entitled "The Last God" is even more emphatic: "The multiplicity of gods is not subject to enumeration but, instead, to the inner richness of the grounds and abysses in the site of the moment for to lighting up and concealment of the intimation of the last god."[25] Heidegger's counter-suggestion seems to be that, rather than a multiplicity of gods, there is a multiplicity of possible intimations of one and the same last god. The following passage suggests why:

> Yet what if the last god must be so named, because the decision about the gods ultimately leads under and among them and so raises to the highest the essence of the uniqueness of the Godhead.[26]

Suppose that there were a multiplicity of gods. What makes them all *divine*? Presumably it is in virtue of a distinct divine essence or Godhead that they share. But since the shared Godhead is what makes the gods divine by pervading them with divinity, the Godhead itself is really the only god and the so-called "gods" are merely different ontological conditions fully pervaded by the Godhead that is not the same as any one of them.[27] What

---

23. An additional consequence is that when the ontological condition (e.g., total nonbeing) with which a particular god is identical does not obtain, then neither does the god. Gods can come to pass and pass away. The crucial question of what makes all of these gods *divine* will be taken up shortly.

24. Heidegger, *Contributions to Philosophy*, 231.

25. Heidegger, *Contributions to Philosophy*, 326.

26. Heidegger, *Contributions to Philosophy*, 322.

27. Nicholas of Cusa raises a parallel objection to polytheism: "All who have every worshiped a plurality of gods have supposed there to be deity. For in all the gods, they

leads under and among the gods leads to "the essence of the uniqueness of the Godhead" as the one and only last god.

A difficulty with the divinity as essential nothingness proposal we described in chapter 7 is that it either unacceptably lapses back into metaphysics by subordinating divinity to metaphysically prior modal principles or it implausibly grounds all modality in the "fissure" between *Da-sein* and *beyng*. The Christological proposal circumvents this difficulty by explicating how modality arises from divinity's doubly converse relationship to the different ontological conditions which are the circumstances of its appearing. A given ontological condition is possible yet not actual just in case divinity is conversely beyond it and is not conversely opposite to it.[28] A condition is both possible and actual—i.e., contingent—just in case divinity is both conversely beyond and conversely opposite to it while also fully pervading it.[29] Necessity and impossibility are not absolute but relative: condition A (e.g., an essential occurrence of *beyng*) cannot obtain without condition B (e.g., *Da-sein*), so that B is necessary relative to A, just in case divinity is both conversely beyond and conversely opposite to A only if divinity is also both conversely beyond and conversely opposite to B. Condition C (e.g., total nonbeing) and condition D (e.g., our current plight) are jointly impossible, so that C and D cannot concurrently obtain, just in case whenever divinity is conversely opposite to C divinity is not conversely opposite to D and vice versa. Possibility, contingency, necessity, and impossibility only apply to particular non-human beings, human beings, the totality of beings, the non-metaphysical event of *beyng*, and total nonbeing, not to

---

adore deity as [one and] the same in [all] its participants. For just as there are no white things if whiteness does not exist, so if deity does not exist there are no gods. Therefore, the worshiping of [a plurality of] gods bespeaks the deity. See Nicholas of Cusa, "On Peaceful Unity of Faith," 640.

28. Divinity is conversely opposite to an ontological condition if and only if divinity fully pervades the condition without being identical with it because divinity is also conversely beyond it. Hence in saying that divinity is (or is not) in converse opposition to something, we are also implying (or denying) that divinity fully pervades it.

29. The same terms can be used to give a theological rendering of the doctrine of creation *ex nihilo*. When there is only divinity and nothing else *ad extra*, divinity is nevertheless conversely beyond yet not conversely opposite to any totality of beings or universe. If at some point divinity is both conversely beyond and conversely opposite to some universe, then the latter is not only possible but also actual and hence contingent. "Creation" of a universe means that God fully pervades and is conversely opposite to it; *"ex nihilo"* means that when a universe is uncreated, God both fully pervades and is conversely opposite to the negative ontological condition of total nonbeing yet is not conversely opposite to any positive ontological condition.

divinity itself as the ground of modality. In its splendid simplicity, divinity is neither conversely beyond nor conversely opposite to itself.

Original Sin Redux: Loving, Leaping, Ecstatic Trembling

Original sin is the plight that as an instance of generic humanity endowed with reason and volition, each one of us is unable to make the leap to genuine human individuality by becoming a perfectly ethical self before a God whom we seek to emulate as much as possible. To become perfectly ethical selves, you and I would have to fulfill every binding moral requirement in any actual or conceivable situation. That we cannot do, for, as Lisa Tessman explains, there are many actual and conceivable moral quandaries in which you and I cannot fulfill all the binding moral requirements but instead must violate one of them. We need not determine the exact origin of this plight in order to recognize it as an inescapable liability of our current human condition. Even if we reject moral values on the basis of Nietzsche and Heidegger's skepticism about how we can regard certain requirements both as morally binding and constructed by us, we are left with no obvious way of becoming existentially concrete selves before God.

Recall that according to Tessman, what we imbue with moral authority are proximate causes of social cooperation. This suggests that we possess a basic desire to live and work together in harmonious community. Tessman goes even further. She relates the case of her friend Celia.[30] Celia's father had been a young Jewish boy growing up in Belgium during the Holocaust. For his own protection, he was sent to a Catholic boarding school. Every week, his mother would come to visit him and bring him cake. One day, she did not arrive because the Nazis had boarded her onto a train and sent her to a concentration camp where she was murdered. Even though these events transpired long before she was born, Celia wishes that she had somehow prevented the Nazis from killing her paternal grandmother and thereby spared her father the terrible experience of abandonment and loss he suffered.[31] Morally, Celia feels that she *must* spare her father even though

30. See Tessman, *When Doing the Right Thing Is Impossible*, 116–17.

31. Thomas Merton shares his own reaction to World War II: "I myself am responsible for this. My sins have done this. Hitler is not the only one who started this war: I have my share in it too" (Merton, *Seven Storey Mountain*, 272). Initially, Merton sounds overly scrupulous in holding himself no less accountable than Hitler for starting the war. A more plausible reading is that Merton deeply wishes he had prevented the war and feels morally bound to have done so, even though he cannot.

it is impossible for her to do so. Yet, as Tessman observes, at a deeper level something else is at work:

> Perhaps we want to be loved in the way that Celia loves her father. . . . Perhaps we need to live in a world in which we can love and be loved in the way that comes with the strong, and automatic, sense that we *must* do certain things, a sense that is paired with the realization that all alternatives to what we must do are unthinkable.[32]

Along with our capacities for reason and volition, a fundamental fact about us human beings that we do not construct is our seeking to give and receive the kind of love Celia feels for her father.

Let us examine this love a bit more carefully. Celia's desire remains as strong as ever notwithstanding the impossibility of fulfilling it. Celia still wishes that she had prevented the Nazis from killing her father's mother, even though doing so would require her to accomplish the impossible feat of changing what happened in the past before she was born. A possible explanation lies in the automatic character of Celia's desire, which does not pause to assess feasibility but immediately sees any other response to her father's suffering as unthinkable. If Celia continues to yearn that she had saved her father even though doing so requires her to accomplish the impossible, then the same yearning persists even if fulfilling it requires her to accomplish any one of indefinitely many possible tasks. For example, Celia still wishes that she had spared her father even if doing so requires her to prevent 100 Nazis, 1,000 Nazis, 10,000 Nazis, 1,000,000 Nazis, or any arbitrarily large finite number of Nazis from killing his mother. What this shows is that the love expressed by Celia's desire to save her father is in an important sense open-ended, unlimited, and boundless.

Sacred scripture proclaims that "God is love, and whoever remains in love remains in God and God in him" (1 John 4:16). It is further implied that God, and thus the love that is God, is not limited or bounded by anything: "Can it be that God dwells with mankind on earth? If the heavens and the highest heavens cannot contain you, how much less this temple which I have built!" (2 Chr 6:18; cf. 1 Kgs 8:27). Viewed through the eyes of faith, then, Celia remains in boundless love—a love unhampered by any number of possible obstacles or by even impossibility itself—and so God remains in her. Divinity not only fully pervades but is the same as the boundless love

---

32. Tessman, *When Doing the Right Thing Is Impossible*, 117–18.

abiding in Celia and that each one of us has or at least seeks to have.[33] Even if I do not yet feel boundless love towards another person or other people, it comes to abide in me when I work to establish familial bonds and ties of lasting friendship with my fellow human beings. Such boundless love is God abiding in me.

But equally rooted in our common human nature is the need to *receive* the kind of boundless love Tessman describes. Sadly, the vicissitudes of ordinary life do not guarantee that anyone else will ever love me like that. Even if I am fortunate enough to have somebody like Celia in my life, it is hardly obvious how my boundlessly loving and being boundlessly loved enables me to make the leap to genuine human selfhood in some manner other than by becoming a perfectly ethical self before God. Does Celia's father become a genuine human self by reciprocating his daughter's boundless love for him? How many others must he boundlessly love and how many others must boundlessly love him in order for him to become a genuine human self? These questions admit of no obvious answers. Only through the double converse that is integral in all divine appearance and epitomized by the phenomenology of the cross do we finally find our footing for the leap.

Insofar as I exist, divinity fully pervades my human existence without being the same as or restricted to it. For divinity is also conversely beyond my existence, in that if some other ontological condition obtains in which my existence is lacking then divinity fully pervades that condition. Thus divinity both fully pervades and is conversely opposite to my existence. Suppose further that God comes to abide in me as the boundless love I have toward some other human being(s). God is the same as my boundless love without being the same as my existence, since I can exist without feeling boundless love towards anyone else. Still, my boundless love is an appearance of divinity itself in me of which I can become aware. Since divinity is doubly converse under any conditions in which it appears to us, God is both conversely beyond and conversely opposite to God abiding me as my boundless love toward some other human being(s). The mode in which God is conversely opposite to God abiding in me as my boundless love is the love for me and all other human beings that Christ expresses through his suffering and death on the cross. Like my boundless love, his crucified love is also open-ended, unlimited, and boundless in scope: Jesus has a strong and automatic sense ("Father, if it possible, let this cup pass from

---

33. The language of abiding is prevalent throughout the Gospel of John.

me; yet, not as I will, but as you will" [Matt 26:39]) not only that he *must* die for us regardless of the number of steps to Calvary or the duration of the execution, but also that he must die for *us* whether we number one million, ten million, one hundred million, or any other arbitrarily large finite number. The boundless love Jesus has for us is God abiding in him. Consequently, my faith in Jesus's boundless love for us equals my conviction that someone else—Christ himself—feels the same divine love towards me that I feel toward some other human being(s). Indeed, through his sacrifice Christ expresses boundless love towards me long before I even begin exist, let alone before boundless love towards anyone else comes to abide in me.[34]

We are now drawing closer to the mystery of the self. Given the double converse pattern running throughout all appearance of divinity, God is not only conversely opposite to but also conversely beyond God abiding in me as my boundless love towards others. Yet the mode in which God is conversely beyond my boundless love is different from the mode in which God is conversely beyond total nonbeing or the essential occurrence of *beyng*. Divinity is conversely beyond these latter conditions by fully pervading some other condition in which they do not obtain. By contrast, divinity is conversely beyond Christ's-crucified-love-for-me-standing-conversely-opposite-to-my-boundless-love-for-others through Christ's resurrection—a condition that does not preclude my existence but in which, as Jesus promises, my resurrected existence also obtains if I believe in Christ. Furthermore, just as the resurrected Jesus appears differently from the crucified Jesus, so I appear differently with Christ in Paradise than I do before.

Heidegger himself speaks of the "excess" in the evolving relation between humanity and divinity:

> The inventive thinking of the truth of *beyng* will succeed only if,
> in the passing by of the god, the empowering of humans to their
> necessity becomes manifest and thus the ap-propriation in the
> excess of the turning between human belonging and divine need-
> fulness comes to the open, in order for the appropriation to show
> its self-concealment as central and the show itself as the center of

---

34. Might *I* reciprocate my boundless love for somebody else by boundlessly loving myself? Or might I boundlessly love and thus be boundlessly loved by myself? Nietzsche counsels: "Liebt euch selber aus Gnade—dann habt ihr euern Gott gar nicht mehr nötig [Love yourselves out of grace—then you no longer need your God]" (Nietzsche, *Morgenröte*, 66 [my translation]). Yet even if somehow I could cultivate towards myself the kind of boundless love that Celia has towards her father, the very boundlessness of my love for myself is Christ, who is God, abiding in me.

self-concealment and to compel the oscillation and thereby make leap forward the freedom toward the ground of *beyng* as grounding the "there."[35]

Our developing theological perspective brings into sharper focus much of what is initially blurry in this passage. The turning between human belonging and divine needfulness is the converse opposition between (1) God's boundless love for us manifested in the crucified Jesus and (2) God's not only fully pervading my faithful existence but also abiding in my boundless love to some other human(s).

The excess of the turning is God conversely beyond the converse opposition between (1) and (2): both in the post-resurrection Jesus, who retains his boundless divine love for us, and in my post-resurrection existence with the risen Jesus, since God not only fully pervades my resurrected existence but also continues to abide in the boundless divine love my existence feels toward some other human(s).[36] Additionally, both the resurrected Jesus conversely beyond (1) and my resurrected existence conversely beyond (2) appear in some different way that cannot yet be fathomed by my pre-resurrection existence in (2). My post-resurrection existence conversely beyond (2) remains grounded in what we have called the clearing work of *beyng*, since no confusions obscure my awareness of divinity.[37] Even so, other confusions about divinity, as well as more effective ways in which my own former confusions about divinity might have been removed, remain conceivable, so that *beyng* itself remains what Heidegger calls the center of self-concealment.

All divine appearance is doubly converse. Thus a converse opposition obtains between (3) the post-resurrection Jesus, who is conversely beyond (1), and (4) my post-resurrection existence, which is conversely beyond (2). Moreover, God is also conversely beyond the converse opposition between (3) and (4): both in the post-resurrection Jesus who is conversely beyond (3) and in my post-resurrection existence that is conversely beyond (4). Again, both (5) the post-resurrection Jesus who is conversely beyond (3) and (6) my post-resurrection existence conversely beyond (4) appear in

---

35. Heidegger, *Contributions to Philosophy*, 328.

36. In Pauline terms, "Love never fails" (1 Cor 13:12), neither in the post-resurrection Jesus who still boundlessly loves us nor in the post-resurrection me who still boundlessly loves some other human(s).

37. As Paul says, "At present I know partially; then I shall know fully as I am known" (1 Cor 13:12)

a different way that cannot yet be fathomed by my post-resurrection existence in (4). Resurrected divinity and divinity abiding in my resurrected existence always stand in a converse opposition they are conversely beyond in a new converse opposition they are also conversely beyond, and so on, indefinitely.

What is my selfhood or full-blown *Da-sein* before the passing by of the last god? Elsewhere in his philosophical commentary on Trakl's poetry, Heidegger writes:

> The simple oneness of pain's converse character comes into pure play only during the journey through the ghostly night, a journey that always takes its parting from the ghostly night. The spirit's gentleness is called to hunt down God, its shy reserve called to storm heaven.[38]

First and foremost, "I" am not a genuine self but merely generic humanity endowed with reason and volition that happens to occur during a particular spatiotemporal stretch constituting my earthly existence and beyond. Yet if boundless divine love for some other human(s) comes to abide in my earthly existence—perhaps through "my" working to establish ties of family, friendship, and fellowship—and if, at the very least, my earthly existence has faith in the crucified Christ's boundless divine love for us and Christ's promise of resurrection, then my earthly existence is initiated into the doubly converse, indefinitely extending "oscillation" or interplay between my humanity and divinity.

My *self* is my existence always following some mysteriously unexpected converse opposition between divinity in Christ and divinity in my existence, where the converse opposition in question lies beyond whatever pre- or post-resurrection condition in which my existence happens to find itself.[39] In addition to being a seeking and preserving steward historically thrown into *beyng's* clearing work of removing conceptual confusions about divinity, my full-blown *Da-sein* emerges as the *hunter* who hunts down God and storms heaven by always encountering surprisingly and

---

38. Heidegger, "Language in the Poem," 189–90.

39. The term "following" in this formulation is deliberately ambiguous: my thrown human existence both *pursues* the newly appearing Christ in converse opposition with my newly appearing divinized existence and *comes after* or *beyond* it in order to pursue yet another converse opposition between newly appearing Christ and my newly appearing divinized existence. One might also say that my existence *chases* itself as it occurs in ever-newer converse oppositions with God in Christ—not only in the way that a hunter chases her quarry, but also in the way a draft of cold water chases a shot of whiskey.

unfathomably new converse oppositions arising between God in Christ and God in my hunted existence which are revealed conversely beyond my hunting existence.[40] Your *self*, your full-blown *Da-sein*, emerges in similar manner—except that the conceptual confusions you have worked to clear away may be different, while the surprisingly and unfathomably new converse oppositions you hunt down which are revealed conversely beyond your hunting existence arise between God in Christ and God in your hunted existence.

As hunters hunting down God in newer and newer appearances both of God's boundless love towards others abiding in our earthly and risen existence and of God's boundless love toward us manifested in the crucified and risen Christ, each faithful human being (*Dasein*) becomes a full-blown human self (*Da-sein*) who is in and indeed is the full-blown pursuit of the last god perpetually passing us by at the edge of an ever-expanding clearing. We can never become perfectly ethical selves who are capable of satisfying all moral requirements in every conceivable situation, but we can become religious selves who cultivate boundless divine love toward others and have faith in Christ's boundless divine love for us. Our quest for our selves thrives on our clinging to such love, not in our adherence to the" moral values" that Nietzsche and Heidegger discard as fictitious projections.

Fully pervading our world while abiding and standing in converse opposition to us, divinity is always intimately near to us at each phase of our quest. Conversely beyond us, divinity is also always tantalizingly rather than frustratingly remote from us at each phase. For we are not trapped in the paralyzing anxiety of having to make a fateful decision about divinity that nothing at it our disposal enables us to make. Instead, the decision for faith thrusts us into the trembling excitement of ceaselessly hunting down what St. Paul aptly describes as our lives hidden with Christ in God (Col 3:3). A thrown human existence that remains indifferent to faith or even decides against it thereby misses out on the thrill of this hunt and thus never attains genuine human selfhood unfolding with and before Christ in

---

40. Kierkegaard defines the self as follows "The self is a relation to itself or is the relation's relating itself to itself in the relation; the self is not the relation but is the relation's relating itself to itself" (Kierkegaard, *Sickness Unto Death*, 13). The Heidegger-inflected conception of selfhood that has just been presented fills in Kierkegaard's schematic definition while removing its initial whiff of circularity. My self emerges through my very existence (which is not the same as my self) not just "relating" but *hunting* a new appearance of my very existence (which again is not the same as my self) in converse opposition to a new appearance of Christ.

God. Such an existence is suitably described by terms ranging from "disappointing" to "pitiful," "pathetic," "miserable," and "damned."

We conclude the present chapter by suggesting possible answers to a pair of lingering questions. Does the leap to the perpetually hunting selfhood of full-blown *Da-sein* unfold in some metaphysical eternity? The conception presented in chapter 5 of Jesus's entire life as a sacred clock against which all religious events are measured as occurring quickly or slowly points to a sense in which perpetually hunting selfhood before God is timeless without introducing any problematic metaphysical conceits. My faithful existence's perpetually hunting down God in itself and God in Christ becomes incorporated into the Jesus-clock as one of its components, similar to how a second-hand perpetually following, catching, passing, and once again following the hour-hand might be added to the mechanism of a standard pocket watch. The movements of the watch's respective components are non-metaphysically timeless, since there is no further temporal standard against which they are measured. Analogously, the movements of the Jesus-clock's respective components—including the perpetual interaction between the risen Christ and the risen human existences that become incorporated into the Jesus-clock, do not occur in time but are also non-metaphysically timeless.

What, at last, of the last god's splendidly simple divinity as something distinct from each individual human being capable of becoming *Da-sein*, each particular non-human being, the contingent totality of beings, the event of *beyng*, and total nonbeing? Heidegger's abstract notion that simplicity (*Einfachheit*) does not consist in the coming together of distinct "relata" or parts can now be injected with definite content pertaining to the last god. The phenomenological dynamics of Christ's crucifixion reveal the doubly converse pattern of divinity as what is always not only conversely opposite to but also conversely beyond any condition of its appearance. If this doubly converse pattern itself derived from the union of independently given parts, then the parts themselves could not already realize the pattern; otherwise, the pattern would consist solely of these independently given parts coming together into unity. Yet because the doubly converse pattern of divinity is already found in any conceivable ontological condition, there can be no independently given parts from whose union the pattern itself could derive. Doubly converse divinity is a holy fractal as simple as it is ubiquitous.

Chapter 9

Against Linguistic Predestination and Scientism

SPIEGEL: You attribute to the Germans a special task?

Heidegger: Yes, in the special sense explained in the dialogues with Hölderlin.

SPIEGEL: Do you believe that Germans have a special qualification for his conversation?

Heidegger: I am thinking of the special inner kinship between the German language and the language of the Greeks and their thought. This is something that the French confirm for me again and again today. When they begin to think, they speak German. They assure [me] that they do not succeed in their own language.[1]

A PAIR OF OBSTRUCTIVE TENDENCIES

As THE JUST-QUOTED EXCHANGE from the 1966 interview he gave to the magazine *Der Spiegel* indicates, Heidegger clearly prefers the German language as the proper medium for thinking. He does not merely take German to be particularly apt for doing philosophy or for facilitating the comprehension of ancient Greek (especially pre-Socratic) texts and fragments. Rather,

1. Heidegger, "Only a God Can Save Us," 62.

Heidegger believes that knowing German is essential to pursuing the sort of non-metaphysical "inceptual thinking" he outlines in the *Beiträge*.[2] In support of his conviction, he appeals to his French colleagues' assurance that they must leave their own language behind and speak German before they can begin to think in the envisioned manner.

Heidegger's "justification" is hardly convincing for a number of reasons. We cannot determine whether Heidegger's French colleagues truly began to engage in inceptual thinking only when they started speaking German. Even if they did, perhaps their inability to think inceptually in French lay not in their native language but in their own inability, just as the fact that some authors can only write great poetry in English doesn't preclude the possibility of writing it in some other language. Maybe others could succeed in beginning to think inceptually in some language besides German. Maybe they already have. Thus it is easy to dismiss Heidegger's attitude as nothing more than German linguistic chauvinism indulged by the fawning remarks of a few French admirers.

However, a much more important issue is at stake here. The question is whether Heidegger's linguistic chauvinism is an indispensable part of the philosophy he presents in the *Beiträge*. If so, then the latter philosophy is suspect to the extent that its linguistic chauvinism remains unjustified. There is a conceptual parallel with the vexed question of whether Heidegger's existential phenomenology in *Sein und Zeit* is inherently National Socialist. If it is, then rejecting Nazism means that we must also reject Heidegger's existential phenomenology. Worse, as will become evident later in the present chapter, even if Heidegger's linguistic chauvinism could somehow be justified, it underwrites a form of linguistic predestination that is directly at odds with the theology of *Streit* we are promoting. To avoid such problems, it will be argued that Heidegger's linguistic chauvinism/linguistic predestination rests upon a metaphysical picture of language that is entirely foreign to the *Beiträge*'s emphasis upon the interdependency between *Da-sein* and the inventive language involved in inceptual thinking.

A second possible obstacle to appropriating key aspects of the *Beiträge* for our theological purposes is Heidegger's dismissive attitude in that work towards natural science. We can begin to appreciate the difficulty by considering a naturalistic objection against the *Streit* theology we have developed and the response to the same objection that the *Beiträge* critique of

---

2. For more on the nature of inceptual thinking, see Heidegger, *Contributions to Philosophy*, 51–56.

science seems to demand. The Christian faith and our *Streit* theological interpretation of it are firmly committed to resurrection as something that has already happened with Jesus in the past and as something that will one day happen with us in the future. The naturalistic objection is straightforward: a phenomenon can be real only if it can be entirely explained by natural science. Since resurrection is allegedly a supernatural phenomenon, in principle it cannot be entirely explained by natural science. Therefore, there neither has been and nor will be any such thing as resurrection.

Ideally, what the proponent of a *Beiträge*-based *Streit* theology needs in order to blunt the naturalistic objection is a principled distinction between (1) science as one practice among others for discovering and explaining truths and (2) scientism, the metaphysical view that science is the only practice for doing so. Only scientism, not science itself, rules out in principle the possibility of any phenomena like resurrection that are not entirely explicable in naturalistic terms. Unfortunately, in his *Beiträge* critique of confusions he takes to be operative in modern technology, Heidegger blurs the distinction between science and scientism. The consequence is that it can seem as if embracing what we have called the clearing work of *beyng* requires us to abandon natural science *in toto*. Many readers might be understandably chary of any theology that demands they abandon science. Fortunately, Heidegger's remarks concerning strangeness and uniqueness can be applied to science in a way that safeguards the latter practice while allowing for strange and unique situations like resurrection falling beyond its scope. We turn our attention first to the anti-scientific tendency of what the *Beiträge* has to say about science.

Concluding Unscientific Postscript?

After describing the plight in which contemporary humanity has been abandoned by *beyng*, Heidegger turns his attention to the role of natural science in the plight:

> Now, however, because in the modern era, and *as* the modern era, truth is fixed in the form of certainty and certainty is fixed in the form of an immediately self-conscious thinking of beings as represented objects, and because the establishment of these fixed forms constituted the foundation of the modern era, and also because this certainty of thinking unfolds in the instituting and pursuit of modern "science," the abandonment of being . . . is essentially

codetermined by modern science, yet indeed *only inasmuch* as the latter claims to be a—or even *the*—normative knowledge.[3]

According to Heidegger, natural science treats beings as objects of representation that possess properties capable of being ascertained with certainty through experimentation. Notice an important nuance in Heidegger's initial remarks about science. Science *per se* does not constitute the abandonment of *beyng*. It is only when science is taken to be the most important or even the sole norm for all knowledge that *beyng* gets eclipsed by the metaphysical distortion that to be is to be a represented object with empirically ascertainable properties. Scientism, not science, is the codetermining culprit in our abandonment by *beyng*.

Yet in passages like the following one, Heidegger's discussion of science takes on an increasingly pessimistic and strident tone:

> Because "science" is not knowledge but, instead, the instituting of correct findings within a region of explanation, then from the adoption of new goals the "sciences" also necessarily undergo in each case new "stimulation," with the help of which they can talk themselves out of every possible threat (viz., every essential one) and can pursue their research with ever more "reassurance."[4]

The quotation marks around "science" begin to sound like disdainful sneers at a practice that yields no real knowledge but merely stipulates its results and misleadingly presents them as if they were genuine discoveries. Heidegger goes on to saddle modern "science" with many of the bugbears he associates with our contemporary plight, from "the effectuation of strict materialism and technicism in Bolshevism,"[5] to the obsession with "organization" in both its "ethnic" (i.e., vulgarly National Socialistic) and "American"[6] (i.e., rampantly capitalistic) versions, to what Heidegger sarcastically derides as "newspaper science,"[7] the business of making the "results" of historiological and other form of scientific "research" available for mass consumption.

All invective aside, what is the philosophical kernel of Heidegger's dissatisfaction with "science"? The sciences' "instituting of correct findings

---

3. Heidegger, *Contributions to Philosophy*, 111.

4. Heidegger, *Contributions to Philosophy*, 116–17.

5. Heidegger, *Contributions to Philosophy*, 116.

6. Heidegger, *Contributions to Philosophy*, 117.

7. Heidegger, *Contributions to Philosophy*, 119.

within a region of explanation" and their ability to "talk themselves out of every possible threat" hint at an answer that Heidegger unpacks a bit further when he writes:

> But a science *must* be exact (in order to remain rigorous, i.e., to remain science) if its subject area is determined in advance as a domain (the modern concept of "nature") accessible solely to quantitative measurement and calculation and only thus guaranteeing results.[8]

Heidegger's complaint is that through calculation and quantitative measurement, each science determines its domain of investigation in such a way that the results of the investigation are already foregone conclusions with no possibility whatsoever of disconfirmation.

This complaint becomes even more explicit when Heidegger asks, "What does the demand for the *repeatability* of an experiment signify?" and then replies, "Communication of the appertaining theory and mode of questioning."[9] To count as count as genuine knowledge, a particular scientific theory must first be tested through repeated experimentation. Heidegger objects that no theory in physics, chemistry, biology, or any other "exact" science—let alone any theory in an "inexact" science like historiology—can ever really be tested, since the experimental setup itself already presupposes the very theory in question.[10] Hence no scientific theory counts as genuine knowledge. The resulting critique of science goes far beyond Paul Feyerabend's view that science is not guided by any general methodology.[11] The very practice of formulating scientific theories and testing them experimentally is claimed to be fundamentally irrational, a *petitio principii* con game in which the evidential dice are loaded in advance to guarantee the desired outcome.

As it stands, Heidegger's critique is unconvincing. Galileo's theory that if air resistance is negligible then objects with different masses will fall at the same rate toward the center of gravity can be tested by dropping 5-kilogram and a 10-kilogram objects from a tower on earth's surface and observing when they reach the ground. Or the theory that the boiling point

8. Heidegger, *Contributions to Philosophy*, 117.

9. Heidegger, *Contributions to Philosophy*, 129.

10. In terms familiar from Karl Popper's philosophy of science, no scientific theory can ever be falsified through repeated experimentation since the experimentation already assumes the truth of the theory. See Popper, *Logic of Scientific Discovery*.

11. See Feyerabend, *Against Method*.

of water at normal air pressure is 100° C can be tested by observing what happens when a pan of water at sea level is heated to that temperature. Both experiments can be repeated numerous times. In each case, setting up the experiment admittedly requires calculation and quantitative measurement, such as that the mass of one object is five kilograms while the mass of the other object is ten kilograms. But none of these calculations and measurements already presupposes the truth of the theory being tested. Merely measuring that the objects' respective masses are five and ten kilograms and that the air resistance in the vicinity of the tower is negligible does not already presuppose that both objects will reach the ground simultaneously when dropped. Or determining that the substance in the pan is indeed water, that the elevation of the pan of water is sea level, and that the water in the pan has been heated to 100° C does not already presuppose that the water in the pan is then going to boil. Nor does the repeatability of the relevant experiment already assume the outcome predicted by the theory being tested. Heidegger has certainly not demonstrated how any scientific experiment involves a *petitio principii*.

Heidegger's concern with the demand for the repeatability of an experiment suggests a somewhat more vague, albeit potentially more powerful critic of natural science. Repeating a given experiment requires duplicating the initial conditions of the experimental setup, such as dropping objects possessing different masses under negligible air resistance from a point relatively near the surface of the earth, the moon, or some other heavenly body towards its center of gravity; or heating a pan of water under normal air pressure to 100° C. Furthermore, the scientific laws confirmed by repeated experimentation, such as Galileo's law for falling bodies or the laws of thermodynamics, are themselves patterns or regularities to the effect that each time such-and-such initial conditions are fulfilled (e.g., objects with different masses are dropped under negligible air resistance towards a center of gravity, water at normal air pressure is heated to 100° C), a definite result follows (i.e., the objects reach the surface simultaneously, the water boils). Even if the objects involved in different experimental setups or applications of a scientific law may vary, they are calculated and quantitatively measured in terms that abstract from their particularity and render them entirely interchangeable for scientific purposes. In this connection,

Heidegger foregrounds science's "Universally valid demonstrability (universal validity" and "objectivity"); representedness and correctness and truth—factuality."[12]

Why might Heidegger find the repeatability inherent in scientific experimentation and the application of scientific laws troubling? In each repetition of a scientific experiment or each instantiation of a scientific law, the beings involved are represented solely in terms of mass, temperature, extension, and other quantitative properties that abstract from the beings' richer phenomenological content. As far as natural science is concerned, it does not matter whether the two falling objects with different masses are rocks or jugs or human beings, whether they are dropped from a castle tower or a skyscraper, whether the water in the pan is a draft taken the Rhine or drawn from a faucet, and whether the sample is heated to 100° C on a gas stove or over the coals of a campfire. Although the beings themselves need not be literally repeated every time a scientific experiment is performed or a scientific law applies, the quantitative properties in terms of which they are represented render them entirely interchangeable. Heidegger's fear may be that the hegemony of scientific methodology in Western culture since the dawn of the Enlightenment makes any distinction between science and scientism otiose. The ubiquity of scientific methodology coupled with the universality ascribed to scientific laws reduces beings to anonymous quantities. It is only short step to the modern technological conception of being that treats beings as nothing more than dispensable and disposable resources in an interlocking system of consumable "standing reserve."[13]

Nevertheless, the *Beiträge* does hint at a line of thinking that would allow for science without scientism. Heidegger characterizes the non-metaphysical event of *beyng* as unique and strange.[14] He understands *beyng*'s uniqueness as its unrepeatability, something historiology and other sciences cannot grasp:

> All "historiology" is nourished by the act of comparison and serves to expand the possibilities of comparison. Although comparison seems to aim at differences, yet for historiology *differences* never become a decisive distinction, i.e., never become the uniqueness of the unrepeatable and the simple, in the face of which historiology

12. Heidegger, *Contributions to Philosophy*, 129.
13. See Heidegger, "Question Concerning Technology," esp. 12–23.
14. See Heidegger, *Contributions to Philosophy*, 161.

(in case it would ever be brought face to face with this) would have to acknowledge itself insufficient.[15]

Concerning *beyng*'s strangeness, Heidegger writes:

> Yet insofar as and as soon as philosophy (in the other beginning) finds itself back to its inceptual essence and the question of the truth of beyng becomes the grounding center, there is then revealed what is abyssal in philosophy, which must turn back to what is inceptual in order to bring into the free domain of its meditation the fissure and the "beyond itself," the strange and the perpetually unusual.[16]

How might the total uniqueness and utter strangeness of *beyng* as a *sui generis* happening aid the *Streit* theologian in overcoming the naturalistic objection to the possibility of resurrection?

Unlike objects with different masses falling towards a center of gravity, a pan of water heated to 100° C, or other repeatable conditions, the event of *beyng*—which includes the work of clearing away conceptual confusions about divinity in order to prepare for a fateful decision concerning the last god—is unrepeatable. Moreover, in accordance with its essential strangeness, the event of *beyng* cannot be represented in terms of quantitative properties that render it interchangeable with other events possessing those same properties. Insofar as "Strangers bring to themselves what is strange with respect of the appropriating event and allow the god to be found in what is strange,"[17] the emergence of full-blown human selfhood through the perpetual hunting down of Christ's doubly converse divinity both abiding in and in contrary opposition to thrown human existence is no less unique and strange than the event of *beyng* from which the perpetual hunt takes its departure.

Since the entire phenomenon consisting of philosophical clarification preparatory to perpetual theophany is strange, unique, and singular, neither it nor the thrown and embodied human existences with which it is inextricably interwoven are repeatable or interchangeable with other phenomena represented as possessing the same quantitative properties. The upshot is that because thrown and embodied human existences are as unrepeatable and non-interchangeable as the overall phenomenon in

---

15. Heidegger, *Contributions to Philosophy*, 118. "The simplicity of *beyng* is marked by uniqueness" (Heidegger, *Contributions to Philosophy*, 371).

16. Heidegger, *Contributions to Philosophy*, 34.

17. Heidegger, *Contributions to Philosophy*, 358.

which they participate, they do not fall wholly within the scope of scientific experimentation and scientific law, thereby leaving open the possibility of their rising from the dead and behaving in other scientifically unpredictable ways. The fact that something sometimes acts in a manner inscrutable to the lens of science does not overturn science, anymore than the fact that something sometimes acts in a manner inscrutable to inorganic chemistry overturns inorganic chemistry. Thus Heidegger's philosophical perspective in the *Beiträge* accommodates a principled demarcation between science and scientism that the *Streit* theologian can then use to turn back the naturalistic objection against the possibility of resurrection.

Few Are Called, Fewer Are Chosen?

According to the basic narrative of the *Beiträge*, through the truth or clearing work of *beyng*, human beings come to the point where they must make a fateful decision that results either in the passing by or absconding of the last god. Although Heidegger does not explain exactly how this decision is to be reached, he has a quite definite idea about how it is supposed to unfold. The human beings who decide about the last god are called "the future ones" divided into three sub-groups. First, there "those few single ones" whose poetry, thinking, and deeds intimate the kind of non-metaphysical clarity required for the fateful decision about divinity. Paradigmatic examples include Hölderlin and Heidegger himself. Then there are "those numerous affiliated ones" who understand and preserve the pioneering work of the single ones so that it begins to take root in a wider public. Finally, there are "those many who are referred to one another" who are gathered around the insights that have been received by the single ones and transmitted by the affiliated ones to form a people.[18]

Curiously, Heidegger describes the future ones as "those strangers alike in heart, equally *decided* for the bestowal and refusal that have been assigned to them" which is "the trembling of the passing by of the decision about the gods, viz., the essential occurrence of *beyng*."[19] He continues:

18. See Heidegger, *Contributions to Philosophy*, 76–77. For a useful overview, see Vallega-Neu, *Heidegger's "Contributions to Philosophy,"* 97–101.

19. Heidegger, *Contributions to Philosophy*, 313 (emphasis added). This passage seems to identify the passing by of the gods with the essential occurrence of *beyng*. But as we have noted previously, elsewhere in the *Beiträge* Heidegger insists that they are not the same. See, e.g., Heidegger, *Contributions to Philosophy*, 207, 346. Heidegger stresses the gods' independence from *beyng*: "'The gods' do not need *beyng* as their proper domain,

The unison of the guiding dispositions is fully attuned only through the basic disposition. In it *are* the future ones, and as so attuned [*gestimmt*] they are determined [*be-stimmt*] by the last god. (On the disposition, cf. what is essential in the lecture courses on Hölderlin.)[20]

It almost sounds as if the future ones are foreordained or predestined by the last god! Whoever comes to participate in the clearing work of *beyng* preparatory to making a fateful decision resulting in the appearance or remaining hidden of divinity is determined by that same divinity, not by human beings. Who are the members of this elect?

Heidegger's reference to the lecture courses on Hölderlin provides a clue. Through Hölderlin's poetic dialogue in "The Ister" with the Sophocles's *Antigone*, the Germans are the ones who are supposed to come into their own:

> The poetry of Hölderlin that has taken on the form of the "hymn" has taken into its singular care this becoming homely in the homely in one's own. . . . What is one's own in this case is whatever belongs to the fatherland of the Germans. Whatever is of the fatherland is itself at home with [*bei*] mother earth.[21]

Heidegger regards Hölderlin not merely as a poet who happens to be German but as the poet of future German *beyng*:

> Yet did not the other poets [Klopstock, Herder, Goethe, Schiller, Novalis, Kleist, Eichendorff, Mörike, Stefan George, and Rilke] too sing and tell of the German essence? Certainly—and yet, Hölderlin is in an exceptional sense the poet—that is, founder, of German *beyng*, because he has projected such *beyng* the farthest. That is, he has projected it out ahead into the most different future. He was able to open up this supremely futural expanse because he brought forth the key from his experience of the most profound need of the withdrawal and approach of the gods.[22]

Taken in conjunction Heidegger's designation in the *Der Spiegel* interview of German as the language of inceptual thinking, these passages make it

---

in which they themselves find a place to stand."

20. Heidegger, *Contributions to Philosophy*, 314.

21. Heidegger, *Hölderlin's Hymn "The Ister,"* 49.

22. Martin Heidegger, *Hölderlin's Hymns*, 201.

difficult to avoid the conclusion that fluency in German is a necessary condition for being included among the future ones of the last god.

Nevertheless, such fluency is plainly insufficient for inceptual thinking, since not only the other poets Heidegger mentions but also the philosophers Leibniz, Kant, Hegel, and Nietzsche were all native German speaks who never achieved the breakthrough to *beyng* and the fateful decision about the last god. Presumably a version of German (perhaps in dialogue with ancient Greek) potentially stands in some privileged relationship to the essential occurrence of the non-metaphysical event of *beyng* and the theophany of the last god. But which version of German, and what is the privileged relationship?

Heidegger does not look to ordinary language, "which is ever more comprehensively used up today and degraded through idle chatter" so that "the truth of *beyng* cannot be said."[23] So the privileged relationship is not the type of correspondence between, on the one hand, grammatical parts of speech in ordinary German with their respective modes of signification (*modi significandi*) and, on the other hand, *beyng*/the appearance of the last god as extra-linguistic phenomena (*modus essendi*) that Heidegger investigates in his *Habilitationsschrift*[24] in connection with Thomas of Erfurt's speculative grammar. Heidegger also implies that the privileged relationship to *beyng* and the last god is not embodied in some new, non-ordinary version of German with artificially formed words like the dense neologisms familiar from *Sein und Zeit*.[25] There is some vague talk of a "sigetics" as a seeking questioning coupled with a studious silence arising out of the essential occurrence of *beyng* itself, but how a German sigetics would look or sound is nowhere elaborated.[26] We are left with the disquieting thought that although some linguistic practice conducted primarily in German

23. Heidegger, *Contributions to Philosophy*, 62.

24. Originally published as *Die Kategorien und Bedeutungslehre des Duns Scotus* and translated in a doctoral dissertation by Robbins as *Dun Scotus's Theory of the Categories and of Meaning*. From these titles, it is clear that Heidegger misattributes Erfurt's speculative grammar to John Duns Scotus. For a critical discussion of some issues in Heidegger's *Habilitationsschrift*, see Dillard, *Heidegger and Philosophical Atheology*, 6–25.

25. See Heidegger, *Contributions to Philosophy*, 62, where he asks whether a new language can be devised for *beyng* and immediately answers, "No. Even if it could, and perhaps without artificially formed words, such a language would not be one that speaks." The subtext is that a language replete with artificial words, like the heavily neologized German of *Sein* and *Zeit*, certainly does not say *beyng*, and devising a new language without them would do no better.

26. See Heidegger, *Contributions to Philosophy*, 62–64.

must stand in a privileged relationship with *beyng*'s essential occurrence setting the stage for the decision about the last god, we have no inkling whatsoever of what either the practice or the relationship is.

This twin uncertainty throws a monkey wrench into the Heideggerian theological perspective we have been developing. The key to overcoming the anxiety of having to decide about the last god who is entirely distinct from any of the ontological conditions available to us lay in the insight that Christ's splendidly simple divinity fully pervades each condition while remaining both in converse opposition to and conversely beyond it. If, however, my decision to hunt down God in, over against, and beyond my thrown existence is determined (*be-stimmt*) by God's inscrutable decision that I participate in the right German linguistic practice standing in the right relationship to *beyng* and divinity, then my initially crippling anxiety is reinstated with a vengeance. For the vagueness of the practice means that I can never be sure whether I have attained it, even if I have mastered German with the fluency of a native speaker. And due to the obscurity of the relationship, I can never know whether it ever obtains between, on the one hand, my speaking and thinking in German and, on the other hand, *beyng*'s essentially occurring and the last god's appearing. No less than Luther's disturbing teaching of *Deus absconditus* or the most extreme form of inscrutable Calvinist double election, Heidegger's linguistic predestination promises to transform the trembling excitement of faith before splendidly simple divinity into a nightmare of doubt.

Fortunately, the linguistic predestination insinuated by Heidegger's linguistic chauvinism already contains the seeds of its own deconstruction. The vagueness of the privileged relationship to *beyng* paving the way to a fateful decision about divinity plays against the vagueness of Heidegger's preferred Teutonic linguistic practice for the "saying" of both *beyng* and divinity. Lacking a precise explanation of what it is about German grammar, etymology, syntax, or semantics that renders the language particularly apt for disclosing these phenomena, it cannot be ruled out *a priori* that the privileged relationship—whatever it is, exactly—could obtain between (1) *beyng*'s essential occurrence followed by the advent of the last god and (2) a non-German linguistic practice in which these developments are lucidly reflected.

Finally, the very idea of a privileged relationship between some preferred linguistic practice and the divinization of *beyng* by the last god is at odds with Heidegger's own repudiation of a certain kind of correspondence between language and reality:

> The yoke (i.e., truth understood as a yoke) is the preliminary form of truth as correctness inasmuch as the yoke is taken as that which *couples* and is not grasped and fathomed as the ground for the correspondence. In other words, ἀλήθεια [*aletheia*, or what Heidegger takes to be the early Greek experience of truth as disclosure against a background of concealment] is genuinely lost.[27]

When a yoke couples two items, they are already available to us apart from one another and only subsequently conjoined through the yoke imposed upon then. In the case of linguistic predestination, the yoke is the privileged relationship, while the separate items are the preferred Germanic linguistic practice and the passing by of the last god prepared through the clearing work of *beyng*.

Elsewhere, though, Heidegger repudiates the foregoing picture of the relation between language and reality as merely another metaphysical distortion. His reason is worth quoting in full:

> Saying is showing. In everything that speaks to us, in everything that touches us by being spoken and spoken about, in everything that gives itself to us in speaking, or waits for us unspoken, but also in the speaking that we do *ourselves*, there prevails Showing which causes to appear what is present, and to fade from appearance what is absent. Saying is in no way the linguistic expression added to the phenomena after they have appeared—rather, all radiant appearance and all fading away is grounded in the showing Saying. Saying sets all present beings free into their given presence, and brings what is absent into their absence. Saying pervades and structures the openness of that clearing which every appearance must seek out and every disappearance must leave behind, and in which every present or absent being must show, say, announce itself.[28]

For linguistic predestination to make sense, we must think of *beyng* and a possible theophany of the last god as independently conceivable phenomena coupled or yoked to a particular preferred linguistic practice via the privileged relationship of correspondence. Yet nothing—including the clearing work of *beyng* setting up a decision about the last god—is

27. Heidegger, *Contributions to Philosophy*, 265.

28. Heidegger, "Way to Language," 126.

conceivable to us apart from language. It is only through the complex welter of our rich linguistic practices that anything whatsoever appears and is thus made available to our thinking.

His commitment to this ubiquity of saying means that Heidegger himself is ultimately not in a position to conceive of any privileged relationship between the German language and the phenomena of *beyng* and divinity. Consequently, his sometime inclination toward linguistic predestination is hoist on his own petard, allowing Heidegger's *Beiträge* philosophy to accommodate an open-ended diversity of linguistic practices that might prove suitable as houses of *beyng* and the passing by of the last god[29] while avoiding any lingering anxiety before the prospect of inscrutable predestination.

---

29. For his famous characterization of language as the house of being see Heidegger, "Letter on Humanism," 236–37.

Conclusion

A Final Reckoning

The old man shook his head. I'm past all that now. Have been for years. Where men cant live gods fare no better. You'll see. It's better to be alone. So I hope that's not true what you said because to be on the road with the last god would be a terrible thing so I hope it's not true.[1]

STREIT THEOLOGY VERSUS *GELASSENHEIT* THEOLOGY

TO BE ON THE road with the last god can certainly seem to be a terrible thing, especially if it requires us to make a decision leading to the last god's either accompanying or abandoning us that nothing whatsoever at our disposal enables us to make. Our goal has been to show how withering anxiety in the face of such a predicament can be transformed into joyful trembling before a splendidly simple divinity fully pervading, conversely opposite to, and conversely beyond everything other than itself. The culmination of our efforts is a *Streit* theology informed by the philosophy Heidegger expounds in *Beiträge zur Philosophie* where the perpetual road we are on with the last god is quixotically its own destination.

A pair of tasks remains to be fulfilled. The theology of *Streit* that we have developed needs to be critically compared with its chief rival, the theology of *Gelassenheit*. Additionally, our *Streit* theology raises several

1. McCarthy, *Road*, 145.

157

lingering questions to which it would be helpful to have clear answers. We now turn to these tasks.

Streit Theology Versus *Gelassenheit* Theology: A Balance Sheet

Unlike *Streit* theology, which associates energized tranquility with the successful elimination of conceptual confusions that distort our understanding of divinity while taking the struggle for clarity against obscurity to pertain to our encounter with divinity itself, *Gelassenheit* theology reverses these phenomenological correlations: our experience of the holy is primarily one of invigorating serenity, whereas the strife between world (disclosure) and earth (concealment) concerns the deconstruction of philosophical confusions about divinity. In previous work within the broad framework of Heideggerian theology rooted in the Christian faith, a provisional decision was reached in favor of pursuing a theology of *Gelassenheit*.[2] Based on a ledger describing some respective strengths and weaknesses of each theological option, the provisional decision was justified on the ground that although the weaknesses of *Gelassenheit* theology can be overcome, the same does not appear to be true of *Streit* theology. Let us revisit three potential drawbacks confronting the latter approach and explain how our version of it avoids them.

Streit theology carries the liability of confronting us with a God who is so perplexing, paradoxical, and even contradictory that our struggle to obtain some measure of clarity from divine obscurity will frustrate us to the point of giving up and losing our faith. In chapter 2, we saw how Luther's *theologia crucis* is vulnerable to this threat when it countenances a God whose revealed will that no sinner is predestined to damnation is contradicted by God's hidden will that some sinners are predestined to damnation. Our version of *Streit* theology does not go so far, since unlike Luther's doctrine of *Deus incarnates et relevatus* versus *Deus absconditus* it attributes no inherent contradictions to the godhead. Moreover, steps were taken to elucidate how our initial anxiety before an uncanny God about which we must decide without knowing how to decide is transformed through Christological insight into trembling excitement as we hunt down both ourselves and splendidly simple divinity fully pervading, conversely opposite to, and conversely beyond our own existence as well as every other ontological condition. To be sure, God is forever uncanny—but in

---

2. Dillard, *Non-Metaphysical Theology after Heidegger*, 71–81.

way that is quickening rather than deadening. Finally, the deconstruction of Heidegger's occasional tendency toward linguistic predestination helped to ward off any resurgence of faith-frustrating anxiety over whether we have mastered the proper linguistic practice and so have come to stand in a privileged relationship with clarified divinity that enables us to undergo a powerful experience of it.

A second potential weakness of *Streit* theology is the risk of what might be called deconstructive overkill. In the absence of a sharp demarcation between metaphysical or other types of philosophical confusion about divinity on the one hand and divine obscurity on the other, the task of attaining conceptual clarity might expand to eliminating the very idea of God itself, ultimately leaving us in a situation that is no less post-theological and post-religious than it is post-metaphysical. However, as has become evident from our discussion of the theological predicament in the *Beiträge*, Heidegger's philosophy in the latter work contains a built-in safeguard against deconstructive overkill: neither the non-metaphysical event of eliminating confusions about divinity nor any other ontological condition Heidegger countenances in his phenomenology enables us to make any decision concerning the last god. Whether or what or how the last god may or may not be is not something that the clearing work of *beyng* can settle by itself. Furthermore, while Heidegger's concept of splendid simplicity provides a glimmer of insight into how the last god can be encountered in each of the available ontological conditions, that philosophical concept must be supplemented with non-philosophical revelation focused on the phenomenological dynamics of the Christ's crucifixion in order to preserve the distinctness of divinity from these non-divine conditions. Only then can humans make the decisive leap into the genuine selfhood of perpetually hunting down God abiding in, conversely opposite to, and conversely beyond thrown human existence.

In passing, it should be noted how the perspective we have presented can do justice to Heidegger's insistence that the non-metaphysical event of *beyng* is finite.[3] There is a straightforward sense in which the work of clearing away conceptual confusions that distort one's understanding of divinity is finite, since eventually it comes to an end. Even if there are other possible confusions one could remove or if confusions one has already removed

---

3. For example: "Therein [i.e., in metaphysical misunderstandings of negativity] appears—quite distantly—ignorance regarding the belonging of the *not*, of the occurrence of negativity, to *beyng* itself; total unawareness of the finitude and uniqueness of *beyng*" (Heidegger, *Contributions to Philosophy*, 93).

could have been removed more effectively, at some point one no longer needs to remove any confusions in order to decide whether or not to hunt down divinity abiding in, conversely opposite to, and conversely beyond one's thrown existence. Deconstructive philosophical analysis then gives way to trembling ardor before limitless divine mystery.

A third liability of *Streit* theology is its apparent inability to accommodate the core doctrinal commitments of Christian orthodoxy including the Incarnation, the Resurrection, and the Trinity. Though *Gelassenheit* theology carries the same liability, efforts have been undertaken to rectify the deficiency.[4] Unless similar efforts are made on behalf of *Streit* theology, it will be obviously inferior to its *Gelassenheit* alternative within the field of non-metaphysical Heideggerian theology in the Christian tradition.

Certainly the Christian advocate of *Streit* theology should labor to dispel any impression that her theological preference is fundamentally at odds with the dictates of her faith. The groundwork for such labor has already been laid at various junctures in the present book. First and foremost, the *Streit* theological proposal developed in chapter 8 has a strongly Christological orientation: only through meditation on the crucified Christ can anxious *Dasein* make a decisive leap into trembling *Da-sein* who perpetually hunts down God and thereby escapes the theological dilemma of having to decide about God without knowing how to decide. The reflections in chapter 9 on embodied human existences caught up in the strange, unique, and singular phenomenon of the last god's theophany unfolding within the expanding clearing of *beyng* were intended to suggest how the possibility of bodily resurrection can peacefully coexist with a healthy respect for natural science.

What of the Trinity? There is nothing wrong with taking the unity of creative, delineative, and captivating emptiness described in chapter 7 as an initial *Streit* theological interpretation of the triune God. The sticking point was the relation of this tripartite emptiness to modality. In light of our findings in chapter 8, the modal properties of possibility, impossibility, necessity, and contingency only apply to non-divine ontological conditions in relationship to the doubly converse divinity that is revealed in the phenomenological dynamics of Christ's crucifixion. Modal properties do not apply to doubly converse divinity itself. Interestingly, Christ speaks of his own body as a temple.[5] Thus like the ancient Greek temple evoked by Hei-

---

4. See Dillard, *Non-Metaphysical Theology after Heidegger*, 131–66.

5. "Jesus answered [the Jews] and said to them, 'Destroy this temple and in three

degger, the incarnate Christ is a delineative cavity who is also creative and captivating. From our parochial human perspective, his doubly converse embodied divinity is the paradigmatic site of Trinitarian emptiness. Consequently, as far as we can say or know, modal properties also do not apply to Trinitarian emptiness but only to the non-divine ontological conditions it conversely opposes and lies conversely beyond. The play of creative, delineative, and captivating holy emptiness apart from the incarnate Christ—e.g., where divinity fully pervades, conversely opposes, and lies conversely beyond the ontological condition of total nonbeing devoid of any human being in which divinity is incarnate—is not something that we can fathom.

Another issue has to do with the emergence of my religious selfhood through my perpetually hunting down God abiding in, conversely opposite to, and conversely beyond my own thrown existence. The theological field in which the perpetual hunt unfolds seems curiously solipsistic. I either do (or at least can) cultivate boundless love towards other human beings, and through faith I am assured of Christ's boundless love towards me. Nothing guarantees that any other human beings besides me will attain the genuine selfhood of full-blown *Da-sein* through perpetually hunting down God abiding in, conversely opposite to, and conversely beyond their own thrown existences. Yet on second thought, perhaps there is nothing untoward about this result after all. Nothing guarantees that *anyone* at all will attain trembling religious selfhood before God. Or if someone does attain it, nothing guarantees than anyone else ever will. Surely, if each one of us is truly free, then conceivably none, only one, or any number of us may freely to decide to embark on the perpetual divine hunt. Naturally, it is to be hoped that as many of us as possible will freely choose to do so.

A last question pulls back from the dizzying perspective of trembling divine perpetuity and returns to everyday life. How can the holy enigma as the *Streit* theologian understands it guide our decisions in ordinary situations? Suppose that I am confronted with a choice between pursuing a lucrative career in the financial industry and becoming a high-school economics teacher. To the extent that I wish my decision to be made under the aegis of the holy, what should I do? *Gelassenheit* theology features a detailed account of holy decision-making.[6] Unless a comparable heuristic is made

---

days I will raise it up.' The Jews said, 'This temple has been under construction for forty-six years, and you will raise it up in three days?' But he was speaking about the temple of his body" (John 2:19–21).

6. See Dillard, *Non-Metaphysical Theology after Heidegger*, 113–30.

available for *Streit* theology, it will be inferior to its *Gelassenheit* alternative on practical grounds.

At least the beginnings of an answer lie in an important structural parallel between the respective experiences that the theologies of *Gelassenheit* and *Streit* identify as the fundamental human experience of the holy. For the *Gelassenheit* theologian, we encounter God primarily through the experience of energized tranquility. When the believer becomes aware of a change that has occurred or might occur in her life, she can hold this change up for holy decision. If she experiences only restless energy or numbing tranquility, then the holy is guiding her to reject the change; if she experiences neither energy nor tranquility, then from the perspective of the holy the change is indifferent. Only when both elements of stimulating energy and calming tranquility come together into a total *Gelassenheit* experience when she reflects on the change in question is the holy guiding her to accept it.

A similar phenomenological complexity informs the experience of *Streit*. *Streit* can be manifested negatively as gnawing anxiety before an uncanny God about whom I must decide without knowing how, or it can be manifested positively as trembling excitement before the intimation of splendidly simple divinity after whom I perpetually leap and so become a true self before God. Once the believer has a firm grip on these different manifestations of *Streit*, she can apply them to any actual or possible changes of which she has become aware in her everyday life so that she may decide in accordance with the holy. If she only feels anxiety when reflecting on the change, then she should reject it; if she feels neither anxiety nor trembling excitement, then she should remain indifferent to it. Only if she feels at least some measure of trembling excitement when contemplating the change should she embrace it as something the holy is encouraging her to embrace.

Tom Rockmore observes that religion serves as one of the deepest sources of Heidegger's thought. Especially in his early career, the Magus of Meßkirch was attracted to an extremely conservative form of Catholicism. At the end of his life, he requested and received permission to be buried in consecrated ground. Yet Heidegger was never able to come to grips with his Catholicism or, more generally, to clarify his relationship to the Christian faith.[7] The gist of the present book is that that even if Hei-

---

7. Rockmore's observation occurs in the documentary *Only a God Can Save Us*, directed by Jeffrey van Davis. See "Martin Heidegger," 7:54–9:09.

degger personally never reached an accommodation with Christianity, his philosophy in the *Beiträge* contains the groundwork for a distinctive form of non-metaphysical Christian *Streit* theology. It is now up to us to continue exploring this and possibly other theological alternatives nourished by Heideggerian insights, so far as God wills it.

Bibliography

Augustine. *Confessions*. Translated by R. S. Pine-Coffin. London: Penguin, 1961.

Beckett, Samuel. *Waiting for Godot*. New York: Grove, 1982.

Biemel W., and H. Saner, eds. *Martin Heidegger and Karl Jaspers: Briefwechsel*. Frankfurt: Vittorio Klostermann, 1990.

Bonaventure. *The Soul's Journey into God*. Translated by Ewert Cousins. Mahwah, NJ: Paulist, 1978.

Bradley, F. H. *Appearance and Reality*. Oxford: Clarendon, 1946.

Bultmann, Rudolf. "Die Eschatologie des Johannes-Evangeliums." *Zwischen den Zeiten* 6 (1920) 4–22.

Camus, Albert. *The Plague*. Translated by Stuart Gilbert. New York: Vintage International, 1991.

Dillard, Peter S. *Heidegger and Philosophical Atheology: A Neo-Scholastic Critique*. London: Continuum, 2008.

———. *Non-Metaphysical Theology after Heidegger*. New York: Palgrave Macmillan, 2016.

———. "Review of *Heidegger and the Question of National Socialism: Disclosure and Gestalt*, by Bernhard Radloff." *The Heythrop Journal* 52 (2011) 164–65.

———. *A Way into Scholasticism: A Companion to St. Bonaventure's "The Soul's Journey into God."* Eugene, OR: Cascade, 2011.

Dreyfus, Hubert L. *Being-in-the-World: A Commentary on Heidegger's "Being and Time," Division I*. Cambridge, MA: MIT Press, 1995.

Faulkner, William. *Requiem for a Nun*. New York: Vintage International, 2011.

Feyerabend, Paul. *Against Method*. London: Verso, 1975.

Friedman, Michael. *A Parting of the Ways: Carnap, Cassirer, and Heidegger*. Chicago: Open Court, 2000.

Guzzoni, Alfred. "Summary of a Seminar." In *On Time and Being*, by Martin Heidegger, 25–54. Translated by Joan Stambaugh. New York: Harper & Row, 1972

Hamsun, Knut. *The Road Leads On*. Translated by Eugene Gay-Tifft. New York: Coward-McCann, 1934.

Heidegger, Martin. *Being and Time*. Translated by Joan Stambaugh. Albany: State University of New York Press, 1996.

———. "Building Dwelling Thinking." In *Poetry, Language, Thinking*, by Martin Heidegger, 143–61. Translated by Albert Hofstadter. New York: Harper & Row, 1975.

———. *Contributions to Philosophy (Of the Event)*. Translated by Richard Rojcewicz and Daniela Vallega-Neu. Bloomington: Indiana University Press, 2012.

―――. "Das Problem der Sünde bei Luther." In *Sachgemässe Exegese: Die Protokolle aus Rudolf Bultmanns Neutestamentlichen Seminaren 1921–1951*, edited by Bernd Jaspert and Rudolf Karl Bultmann, 28–33. Marburg: N. G. Elwert, 1996.

―――. *Die Kategorien und Bedeutungslehre des Duns Scotus*. Tübingen: University of Tübingen Press, 1916. [English: *Dun Scotus's Theory of the Categories and of Meaning*. Translated by Harold Robbins. Chicago: DePaul University, 1978].

―――. *Hölderlin's Hymn "The Ister."* Translated by William McNeill and Julia Davis. Bloomington: Indiana University Press, 1996.

―――. *Hölderlin's Hymns "Germania" and "The Rhine."* Translated by William McNeill and Julia Ireland. Bloomington: Indiana University Press, 2014.

―――. *An Introduction to Metaphysics*. Translated by Ralph Manheim. New Haven: Yale University Press, 1987.

―――. "Language." In *Poetry, Language, Thought*, by Martin Heidegger, 187–210. Translated by Albert Hofstadter. San Francisco: Harper & Row, 1975.

―――. "Language in the Poem: A Discussion on Georg Trakl's Poetic Work." In *On the Way to Language*, by Martin Heidegger, 158–98. Translated by Peter D. Hertz. San Francisco: Harper & Row, 1982.

―――. "Letter on Humanism." In *Martin Heidegger: Basic Writings*, edited by David Farrell Krell, 213–65. Translated by Frank A. Capuzzi. San Francisco: Harper Collins, 1993.

―――. *Martin Heidegger: Basic Writings*. Edited by David Farrell Krell. San Francisco: Harper Collins, 1993.

―――. "The Nature of Language." In *On the Way to Language*, by Martin Heidegger, 57–108. Translated by Peter D. Hertz. San Francisco: Harper & Row, 1982.

―――. *On Time and Being*. Translated by Joan Stambaugh. New York: Harper & Row, 1972.

―――. "'Only a God Can Save Us': The *Spiegel* Interview (1966)." In *Heidegger: The Man and the Thinker*, edited by Thomas Sheehan, 45–68. Translated by William J. Richardson. New Brunswick: Transaction, 2010.

―――. "The Origin of the Work of Art." In *Poetry, Language, Thought*, by Martin Heidegger, 15–87. Translated Albert Hofstadter. New York: Harper & Row, 1975.

―――. *Pathmarks*. Edited by William McNeill. Cambridge: Cambridge University Press, 2009.

―――. *Phänomenologie des religiösen Lebens*. Gesamtausgabe 60. Frankfurt am Main: Vittorio Klostermann, 1992.

―――. "Phenomenology and Theology." In *Pathmarks*, edited by William McNeill, 39–62. Translated by James G. Hart and John C. Maraldo. Cambridge: Cambridge University Press, 2009.

―――. *Phenomenology of Religious Life*. Translated by Matthias Fritsche and Jennifer Anna Gosetti-Ferencei. Bloomington: Indiana University Press, 2010.

―――. "'. . . Poetically Man Dwells . . .'" In *Poetry, Language, Thought*, by Martin Heidegger, 211–29. Translated Albert Hofstadter. New York: Harper & Row, 1975.

―――. "The Question Concerning Technology." In *The Question Concerning Technology and Other Essays*, translated by William Lovitt, 3–35. New York: Harper & Row, 1977.

―――. "The Thing." In *Poetry, Language, Thought*, by Martin Heidegger, 63–186. Translated Albert Hofstadter. New York: Harper & Row, 1975.

———. "The Thinker as Poet." In *Poetry, Language, Thought*, by Martin Heidegger, 3–14. Translated Albert Hofstadter. New York: Harper & Row, 1975.

———. "Time and Being." In *On Time and Being*, by Martin Heidegger, 1–24. Translated by Joan Stambaugh. New York: Harper & Row, 1972.

———. "The Way to Language." In *On the Way to Language*, by Martin Heidegger, 111–36. Translated by Peter D. Hertz. San Francisco: Harper & Row, 1982.

———. "What is Metaphysics?" In *Martin Heidegger: Basic Writings*, edited by David Farrell Krell, 89–110. Translated by David Farrell Krell. San Francisco: Harper & Row, 1993.

Hölderlin, Friedrich. "'Was ist Gott. . .?' ('What is God. . .?')." In *Friederich Hölderlin: Selected Poems and Fragments*, edited by Jeremy Adler, 270–71. Translated by Michael Hamburger. London: Penguin, 1998.

Husserl, Edmund. *Cartesian Meditations*. Translated by Dorion Cairns. The Hague: Martinus Nijoff, 1960.

Idhe, Don. *Experimental Phenomenology: Multistabilities*. Albany: SUNY Press, 2012.

Jaspert, Bernd, ed. *Sachgemässe Exegese: Die Protokolle aus Rudolf Bultmanns Neutestamentlichen Seminaren 1921–1951*. Marburg: N. G. Elwert, 1996.

Kafka, Franz. *Der Prozess*. Fischer: Frankfurt am Main, 1964.

Kelly, John. *The Great Mortality: An Intimate History of the Black Death, the Most Devastating Plague of All Time*. New York: Harper Perennial 2005.

Kierkegaard, Søren. *The Concept of Anxiety*. Translated by Alastair Hannay. New York: Liveright, 2014.

———. *Fear and Trembling*. Translated by Howard V. Hong and Edna H. Hong. Princeton: Princeton University Press, 1983.

———. *The Sickness Unto Death: A Christian Psychological Exposition for Upbuilding and Awakening*. Translated by Howard V. Hong and Edna H. Hong. Princeton: Princeton University Press, 1980.

Killy, Walther. "Nachwort." In *Der Prozess*, by Franz Kafka, 166–68. Fischer: Frankfurt am Main, 1964.

Kittredge, William, ed. *The Portable Western Reader*. New York: Penguin, 1997.

Luther, Martin. "The Bondage of the Will." In *Erasmus and Luther: Discourse on Free Will*, edited by Ernest F. Winter, 85–120. Translated by Ernst F. Winter. New York: Continuum, 1995.

———. *D. Martin Luthers Werke: Kritische Gesamtausgabe*. Weimar: Hermann Böhlaus, 1883–2009.

———. *Luther's Works*. Edited by Jaroslav Pelikan and Helmut T. Lehmann. Vol. 1. Philadelphia: Fortress, 1955.

———. *Table Talk*. Translated by William Hazlitt. Grand Rapids, MI: Christian Classics Ethereal Library, 2004. Online. https://reformed.org/wp-content/uploads/2019/04/MartinLutherTableTalk.pdf.

Maly, Kenneth. "Turnings in Essential Swaying and the Leap." In *Companion to Heidegger's "Contributions to Philosophy,"* edited by Charles E. Scott, et al., 150–70. Bloomington: Indiana University Press, 2001.

"Martin Heidegger: Only a God Can Save Us." Youtube video, 14:52. Posted by Jeffrey van Davis, November 6, 2011. https://www.youtube.com/watch?v=CYtPUW_GGw0.

McCarthy, Cormac. *The Road*. New York: Alfred A. Knopf, 2006.

McGrath, Alister. *Luther's Theology of the Cross*. Oxford: Blackwell, 1990.

McGrath, S. J. *The Early Heidegger and Medieval Philosophy: Phenomenology for the Godforsaken*. Washington, DC: Catholic University Press of America, 2006.

———. *Heidegger: A (Very) Critical Introduction*. Grand Rapids: Eerdmans, 2008.

Merton, Thomas. *The Seven Storey Mountain*. New York: Harcourt Brace, 1998.

Milton, John. *Areopagitica and Other Prose Works*. Edited by Jim Miller. Mineola: Dover, 2016.

Neske, Günther, ed. *Erinnerung an Martin Heidegger*. Pfullingen: Günther Neske, 1977.

Nicholas of Cusa. "On Learned Ignorance." In vol. 1 of *Complete Philosophical and Theological Treatises of Nicholas of Cusa*, edited by Jasper Hopkins, 1–150. Translated by Jasper Hopkins. Minneapolis: Arthur J. Banning, 2001.

———. "On Peaceful Unity of Faith." In vol. 1 of *Complete Philosophical and Theological Treatises of Nicholas of Cusa*, edited by Jasper Hopkins, 633–70. Translated by Jasper Hopkins. Minneapolis: Arthur J. Banning, 2001.

Nietzsche, Friedrich. *Morgenröte: Gedanken über die moralischen Vorurteile*. Munich: Wilhem Goldmann, 1973.

———. *The Will to Power*. Translated by Anthony M. Ludovici. New York: Barnes and Noble, 2006.

Pöggler, Otto. "'Historicity' in Heidegger's Late Work." Translated by J. N. Mohanty. *Southwestern Journal of Philosophy* 4 (1973) 53–72.

Polt, Richard. *The Emergency of Being: On Heidegger's Contributions to Philosophy*. Ithaca: Cornell University Press, 2006.

———. "The Event of Enthinking the Event." In *Companion to Heidegger's "Contributions to Philosophy,"* edited by Charles E. Scott et al., 81–104. Bloomington: Indiana University Press, 2001.

Popper, Karl. *The Logic of Scientific Discovery*. London: Hutchinson, 1959.

Pseudo-Dionysius. "On Divine Names." In vol. 1 of *The Works of Dionysius the Areopagite*, edited by John Parker, 1–127. Translated by John Parker. London: James Parker, 1897.

———. "On the Heavenly Hierarchy." In vol. 2 of *The Works of Dionysius the Areopagite*, edited by John Parker, 1–66. Translated by John Parker. London: James Parker, 1897.

Quine, W. V. "Ontology and Ideology." *Philosophical Studies* 2 (1951) 11–15.

———. "Ontology and Ideology Revisited." *Journal of Philosophy* 80 (1983) 499–502.

———. *Word and Object*. Cambridge, MA: MIT Press, 1988.

Rogers, Pattiann. "Why Divinity Remains Lost." In *The Portable Western Reader*, edited by William Kittredge, 518–19. New York: Penguin, 1997.

Rosemann, Phillip W. *Understanding Scholastic Thought with Foucault*. New York: St. Martin's, 1999.

Safranski, Rüdiger. *Martin Heidegger: Between Good and Evil*. Translated by Ewald Osers. Cambridge, MA: Harvard University Press, 1998.

Scharr, Adam. *Heidegger's Hut*. Cambridge, MA: MIT Press, 2006.

Schmidt, Dennis J. "Strategies for a Possible Reading." In *Companion to Heidegger's "Contributions to Philosophy,"* edited by Charles E. Scott et al., 32–47. Bloomington: Indiana University Press, 2001.

Sciascia, Leonardo. *La Sicile comme métaphore*. Paris: Editions Stock, 1979.

Scott, Charles E., et al, eds. *Companion to Heidegger's "Contributions to Philosophy."* Bloomington: Indiana University Press, 2001.

Sheehan, Thomas, ed. *Heidegger: The Man and the Thinker*. New Brunswick: Transaction, 2010.

Sorabji, Richard. *Time, Creation, and Eternity: Theories in Antiquity and the Early Middle Ages*. Chicago: University of Chicago Press, 1988.

Tessman, Lisa. *When Doing the Right Thing Is Impossible*. Oxford: Oxford University Press, 2017.

Trakl, Georg. *Die Dichtungen. Gesamtausgabe mit einem Anhang: Zeugnisse und Erinnerungen*. Salzburg: Otto Müller, 1938.

Vallega, Alejandro. "'Being-Historical Thinking' in Heidegger's *Contributions to Philosophy*." In *Companion to Heidegger's "Contributions to Philosophy*," edited by Charles E. Scott, et al., 48–65. Bloomington: Indiana University Press, 2001.

Vallega-Neu, Daniela. *Heidegger's "Contributions to Philosophy": An Introduction*. Bloomington: Indiana University Press, 2003.

Welte, Bernhard. "Erinnerung an ein spätes Gespräch." In *Erinnerung an Martin Heidegger*, edited by Günther Neske, 251. Pfullingen: Günther Neske, 1977.

Wittgenstein, Ludwig. *On Certainty*. Translated by Denis Paul and G. E. M. Anscombe. New York: Harper & Row, 1972.

Wolfe, Judith. *Heidegger's Eschatology: Theological Horizons in Martin Heidegger's Early Work*. Oxford: Oxford University Press, 2013.

Index

Made in the USA
Monee, IL
10 October 2020